YOUR WORDS

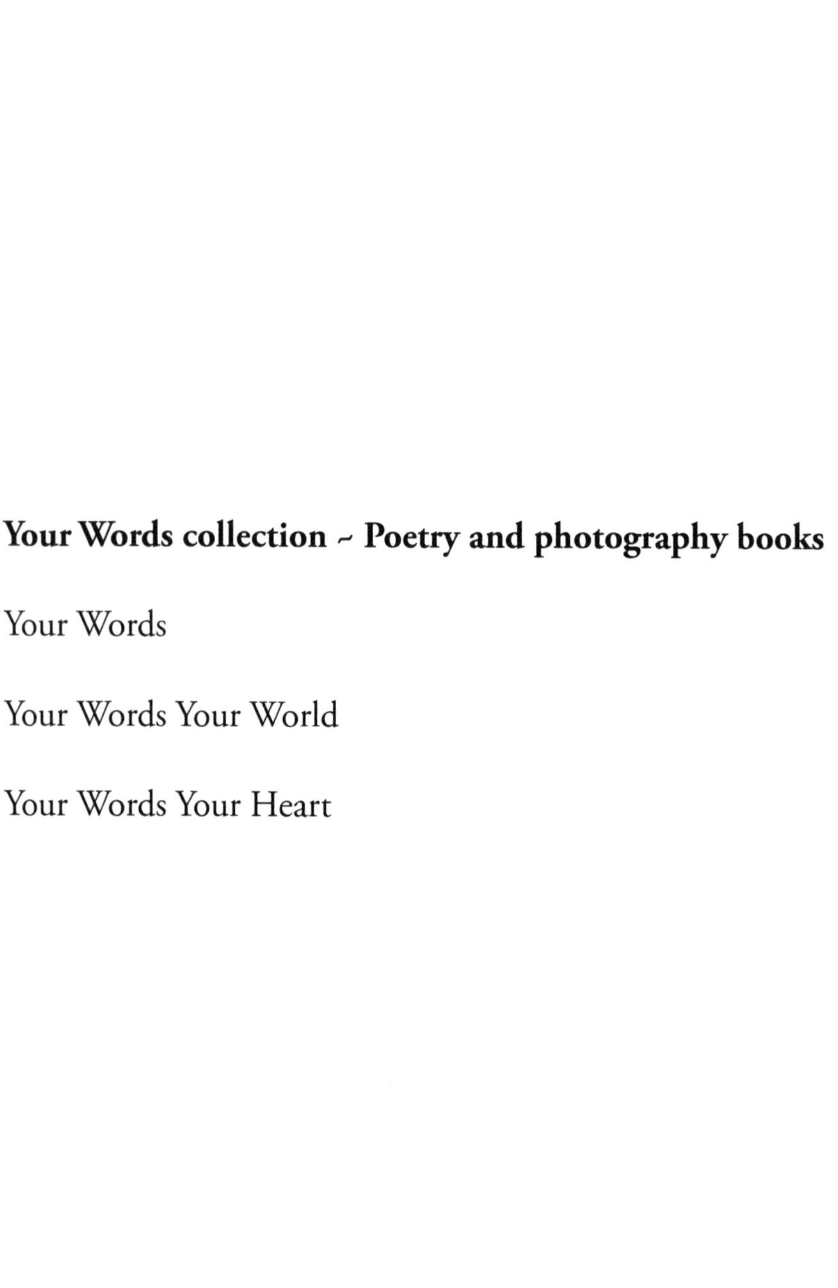

Your Words collection ~ Poetry and photography books

Your Words

Your Words Your World

Your Words Your Heart

Your Words

Louise Bélanger

Published by Abundance Books LLC
Kalamazoo, Michigan

www.abundance-books.com

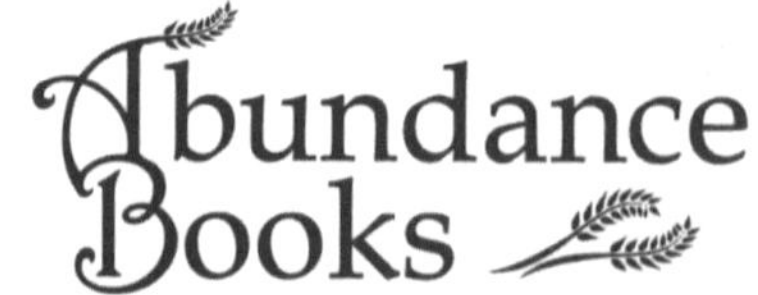

To God

To John and Fatima, new friends I cherish

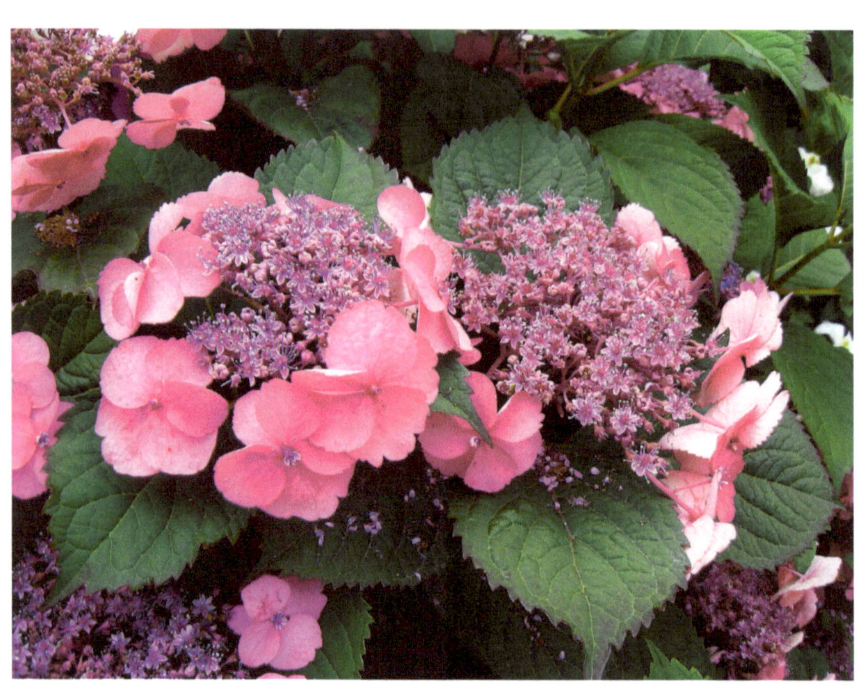

Poems, stories, photographs
All gifts from God

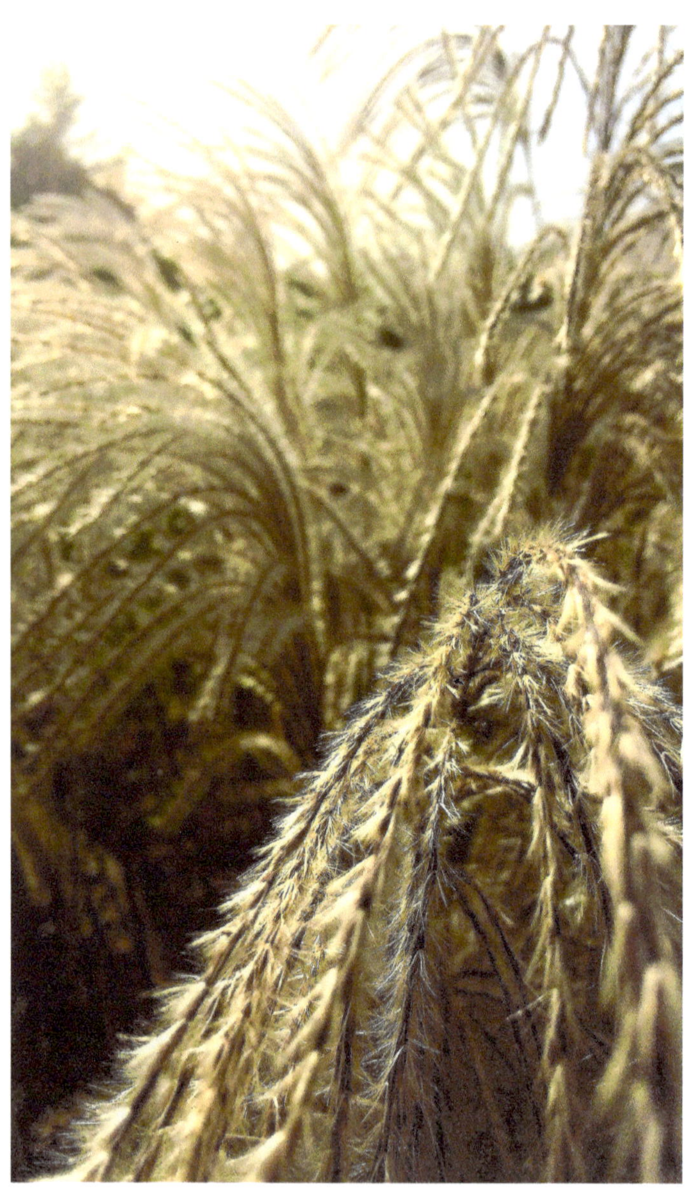

Poems

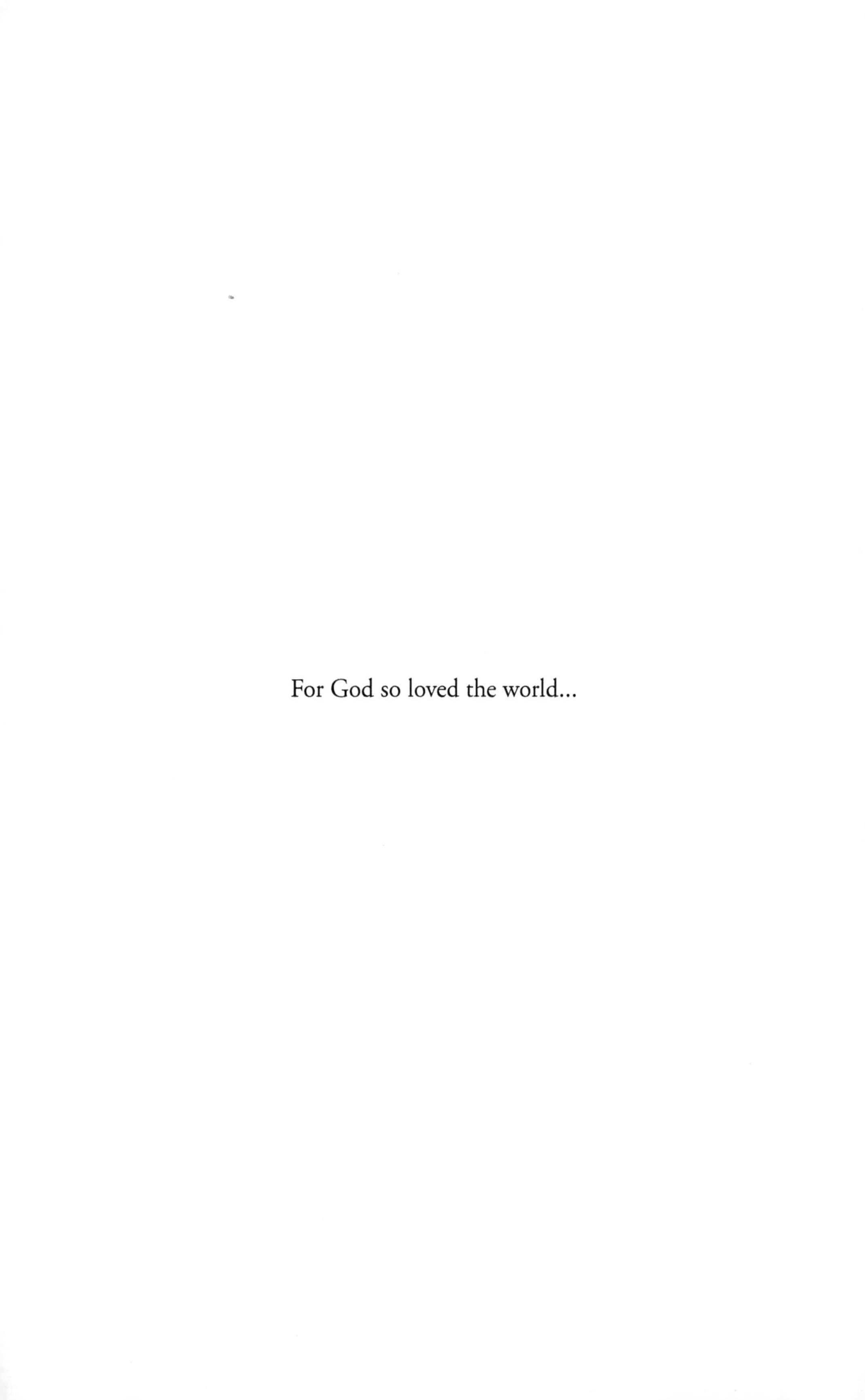

For God so loved the world...

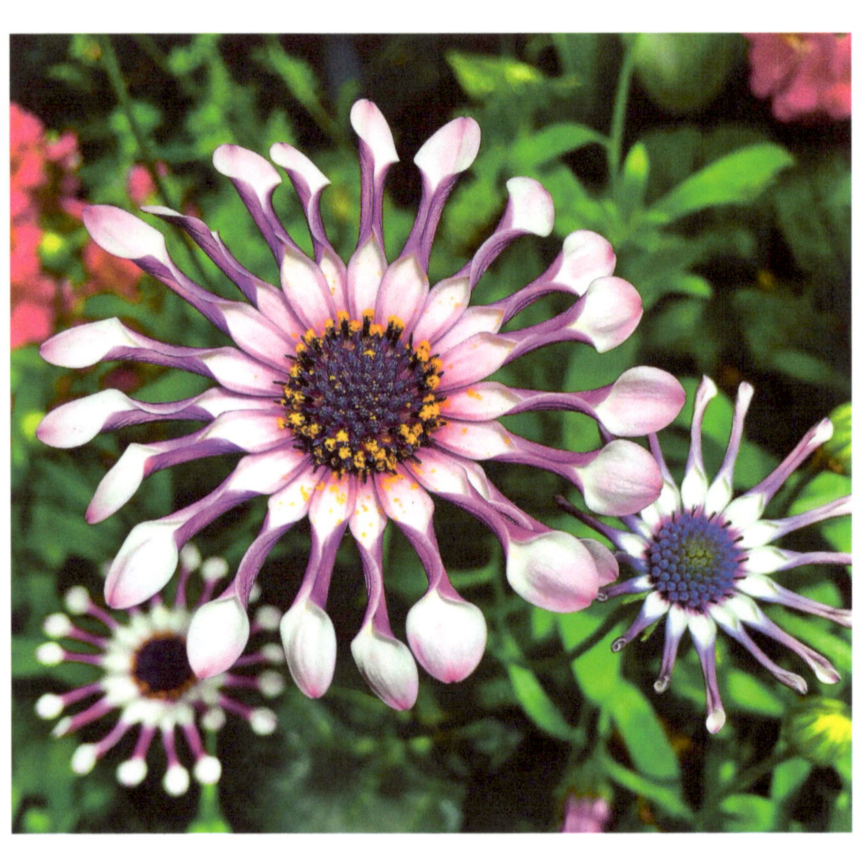

I will again...

I will again feel safe and happy in this world
I will again feel the warmth of an embrace from a friend
I will again feel the sun on my face and close my eyes in
delight, not fearing being too close to someone

I will again...dance to music with no care in the world!
I will again...

April 19 - J'en ai assez ! I've had enough! I have been stuck at
home for more than a month now
I want to be happy again!

April 20 - Covid-19, you evil thing, you ripped my life apart!
You took my job, you took my friends, you invaded my world
and filled me with dread
You stole my joy, you stole my peace, you caused havoc and
filled me with fears

No more joy in the morning
No more pleasure walking outside
No more dancing to music without a care in the world

You stole my sleep, you disrespected my plans, and you broke
my heart

Oh, I know what you say, "But Louise, you let me."
And I say "Yes, you are right! I let you break my defences, and
you moved right in."

But now I say, "It's quite enough!"

Covid-19, you evil thing
You didn't steal everything from me
I'm still me

Whatever makes me, me, still exists
You can't take it away from me! It's not yours to take
I am still the same person inside

You can't take my character
You can't take what I like or dislike
You did break my heart, but you didn't take it
You couldn't because it's not yours to take
It belongs to God and so do I

Covid-19, you evil thing, you are invisible to my eyes
But I choose to see your invisibleness in a cloud in the middle
of a field

You are all alone in the mist
Yes! You!
You are the one who is alone, not me
I may be alone in my apartment confined to my walls
But in this moving image
The image I decided to implant in my mind
You are the one alone surrounded by an army of crushing
soldiers circling you
I am part of these soldiers

We have surrounded you, you have nowhere to go, we're
marching towards you and we're crushing you; you will
suffocate

We're fighting back!

Covid-19, you evil thing, do you exist because of our foolish
ways?
Did we overstep and disrupt a law, disrespecting a balance in
nature?
A scale in the world we unbalanced somehow

Are we to blame?

Maybe
Most probably!
Our ways have helped you grow, have helped you spread and
become deadly

Nevertheless, we're marching on
You stole a lot from us, but you did not steal who we are
And you did not steal our God

The lessons we are to learn, He will teach us
The army in my moving image is God's army and I have joined
in

Each day, Covid-19, you evil thing, you will feel your strength
die as we march on
There is no exit for you
You will be crushed to nothing
God's army is undefeated
You will stop stealing from me, from us!

I will again feel safe and happy in this world, my world
I will again feel the warmth and the joy of an embrace from a
loved one
I will again feel the sun on my face and close my eyes in delight
not fearing being too close to someone

I will again...dance to music with no care in the world!
I will again...

April 20, 2020

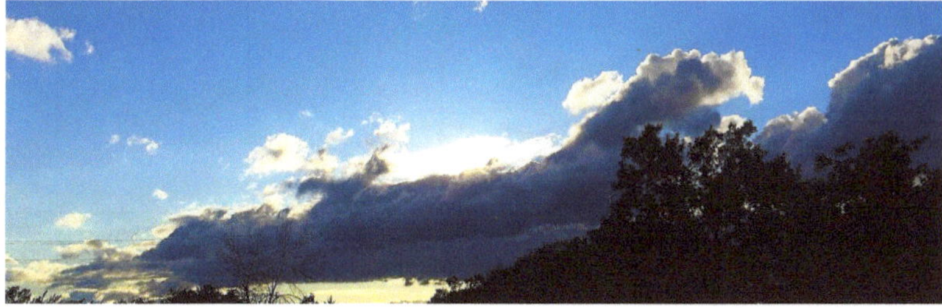

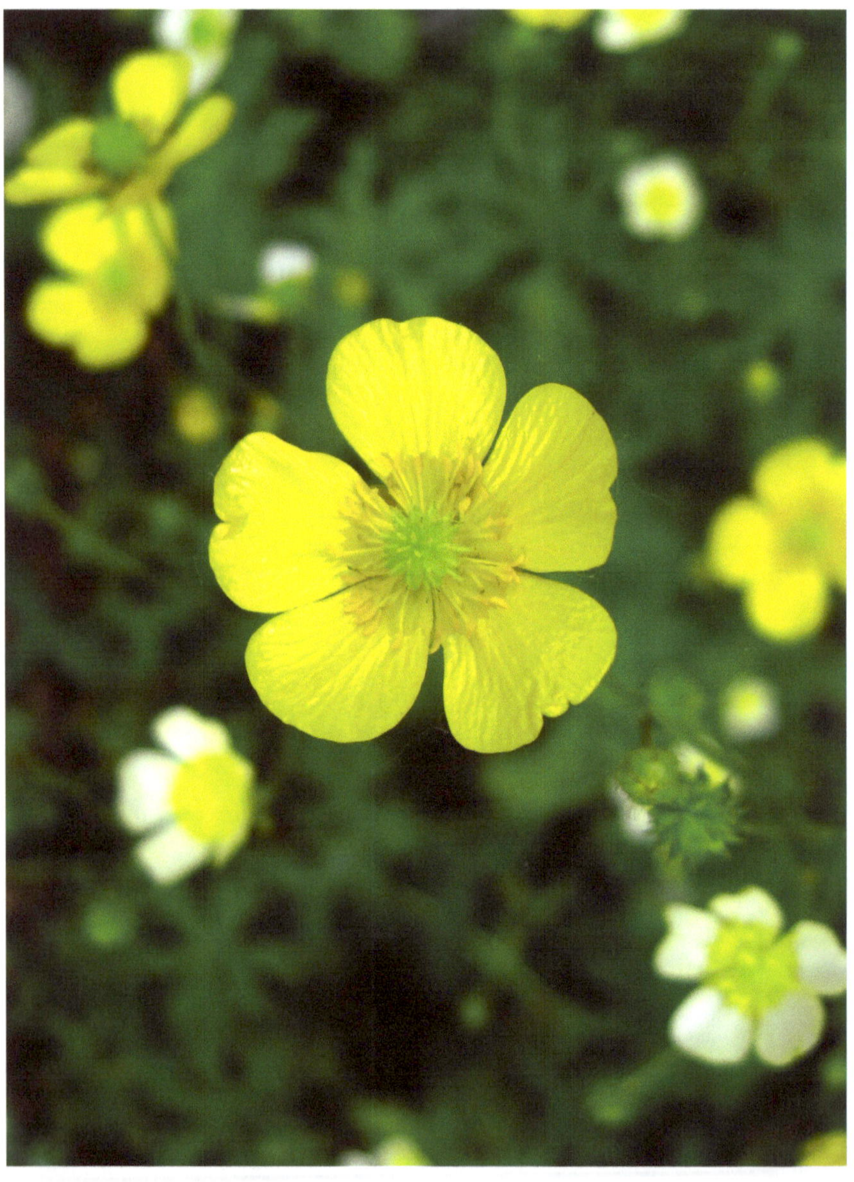

Can't you stop?

Can't you stop?
Stop long enough to see

See the weaving pattern of a dancing snowflake
See the yellow petals of a gold button flower
See the jumping drops of a cascading river

Can you stop...and see Me

Do you see the world I've created?
Nature and fields, oceans and people, they all come from Me

Do you see your heart?
Do you see I live here?
Do you see the gifts?
Do you see the faith and the love I came with?

Can't you stop and see that through My Son you are free...

April 30, 2020

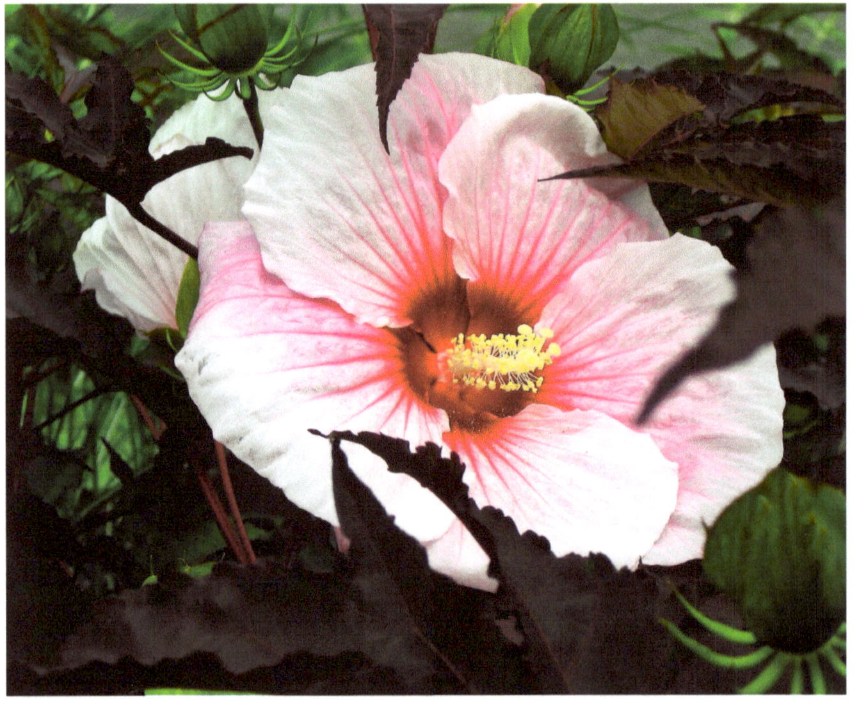

Oh please tell me again!

I'm fighting sadness and I barely sleep
I purchased some masks since I'm told it's best

I bought them to help but all I can see
Something I wish that I wouldn't

Fear... I don't want you here

Fear of getting, fear of spreading

For most of my life, danger, it appears
Had always chooses to remain everywhere but here

Oh I know you exist, everywhere but here
Felt safe in my country, felt safe in my city

Now I'm told it's best
Since some disagree
To respect each other's personal sphere

I don't want to wear them
Why can't people agree?

Oh please tell me again!
Yes, God, tell me again

Yes, Louise, I'm still here
I still protect, I still hold you near
I still kill all your fears; wipe away all your tears

Yes, Louise, I'm still here
I still rule, I still heal
I still save; I still love what is dear

And I will again help you see... I Am near, I Am still here!

May 1, 2020

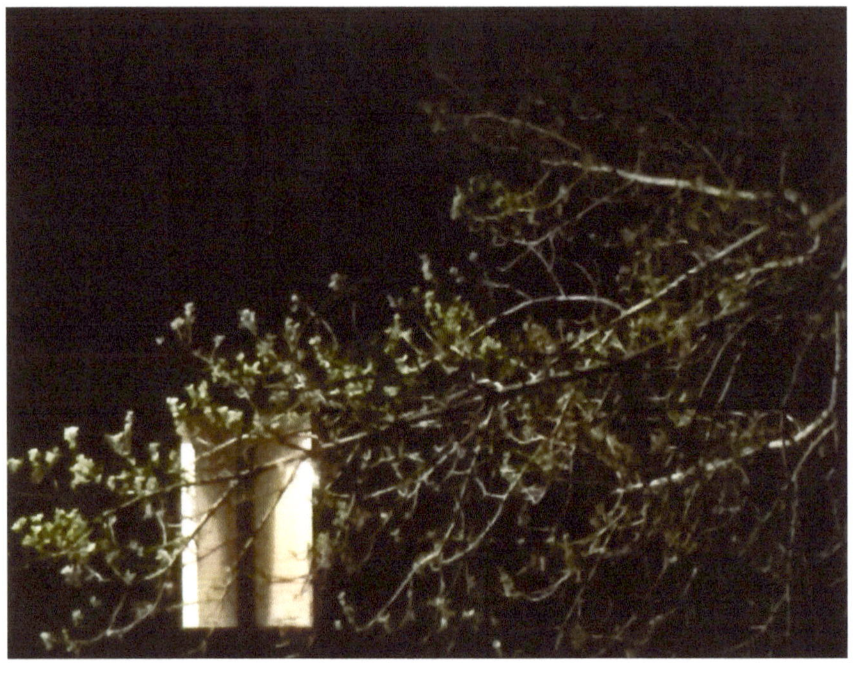

And I'll run up the hill!

I stay in to obey
I stay in to avoid being ill
I stay in to remain hidden from this thing
But I feel like I stopped living

I stay in to avoid dying, but isn't it what is happening a little bit
each day

Each day I miss...

Walking outside to go meet some friends
Seeing a cat that plays with some leaves and stop to come for a
caress
Laughing so hard my stomach aches
Hearing the roaring of the sea
Welcoming new people to my country
Embracing the little girl that decided my lap was where she
wanted to sit that day

The birds outside don't seem to realize
"Don't you know it is best to stay inside?" I feel like saying
"Why are you flying so close to each other, you're not from the
same family?
Didn't you hear it's dangerous?"

...Or is it just us? And you can still freely fly while I stay inside

You know what?
I'm tired of this valley
God, can I go up the hill now?

What do You say?

Until You say, "Yes!" I stay in my valley

I don't want to feel like I'm slowly dying
I will do all these things I enjoyed
When I was happy that I was inside
All these days that I was not working, and it was pouring
outside

And soon...when You do say, "Yes, you can go up the hill
now!"
I'll leave this valley
And I'll run up the hill!

May 4, 2020

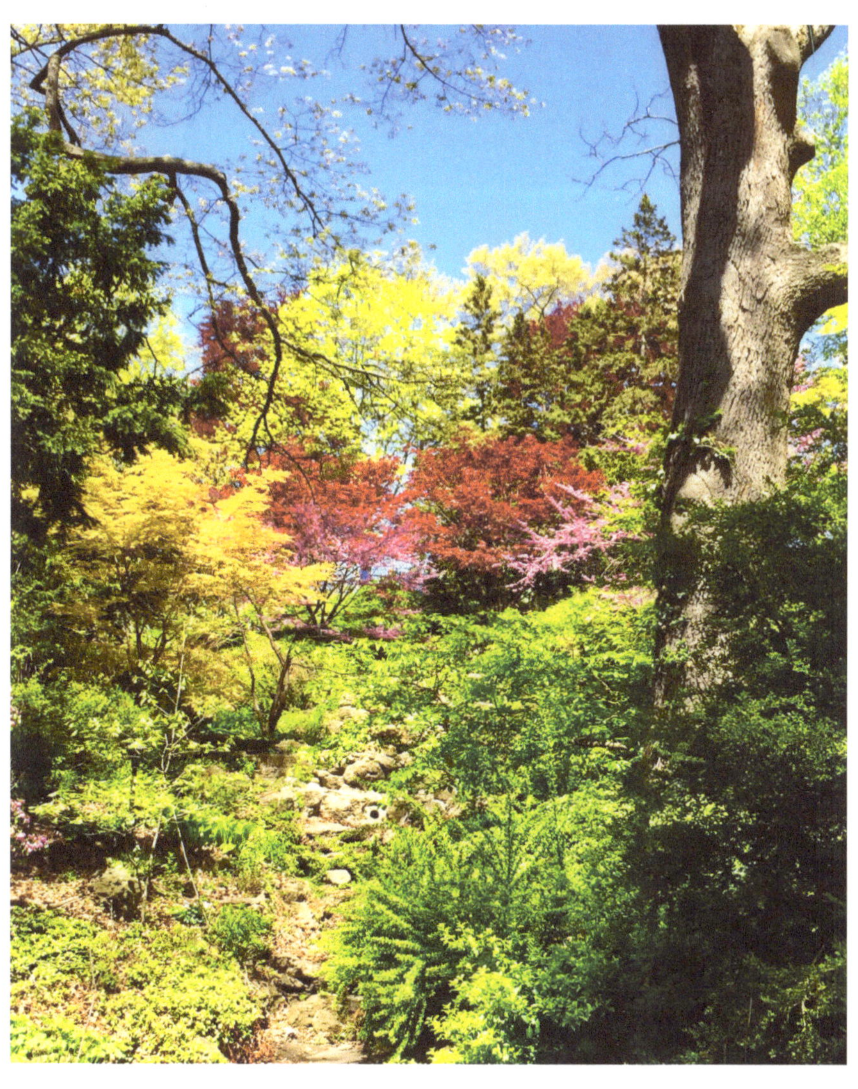

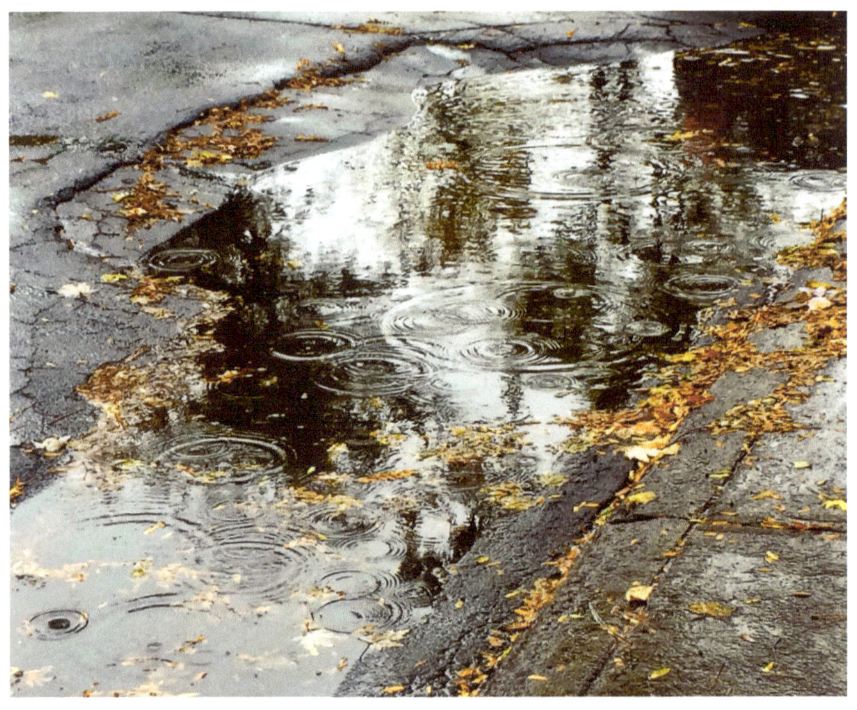

You forgot I was also your friend

I came to help, and I became your friend
I became sick, and I needed help
Somehow you forgot I needed a friend

I got better so I came back to help
Then you remembered I was also your friend

A big monster didn't come to help

So as to not get sick I was told; "Don't come to help."
And once again, you forgot I was also your friend

You called 'cause you needed help
I did, 'cause I'd come to help and became your friend

But once again, you forgot...so God gave me new friends

May 5, 2020

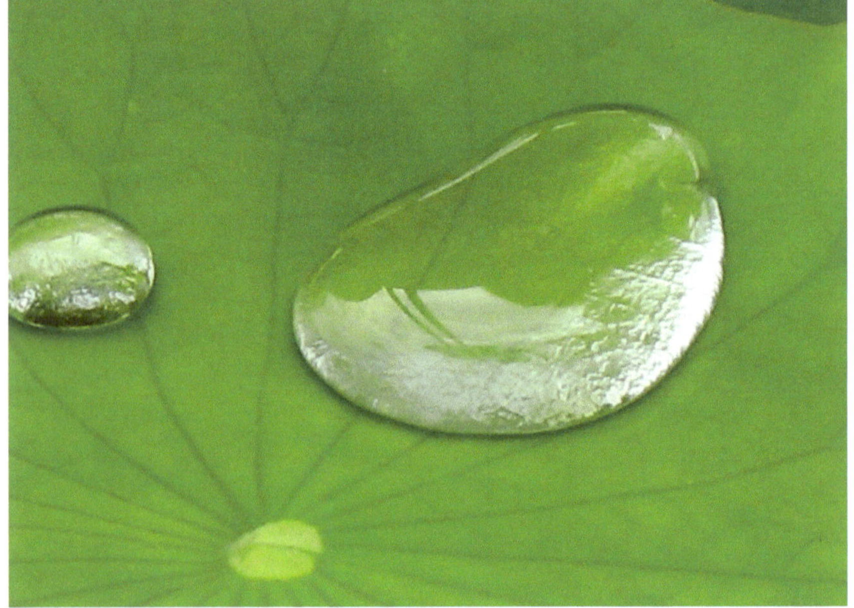

Water

When all you do is put out fires instead of building
You will keep running with water in your hand

Take time to pause

Has God placed people in your life you said you cared about?

Have you taken the time to be interested in something that is
dear to them?
Have you taken some time to spend with them?
Have you given your time to build something beautiful with
them?

A friendship

Then I guess, you're not building
And I see more than just water slipping away between your
fingers

May 7, 2020

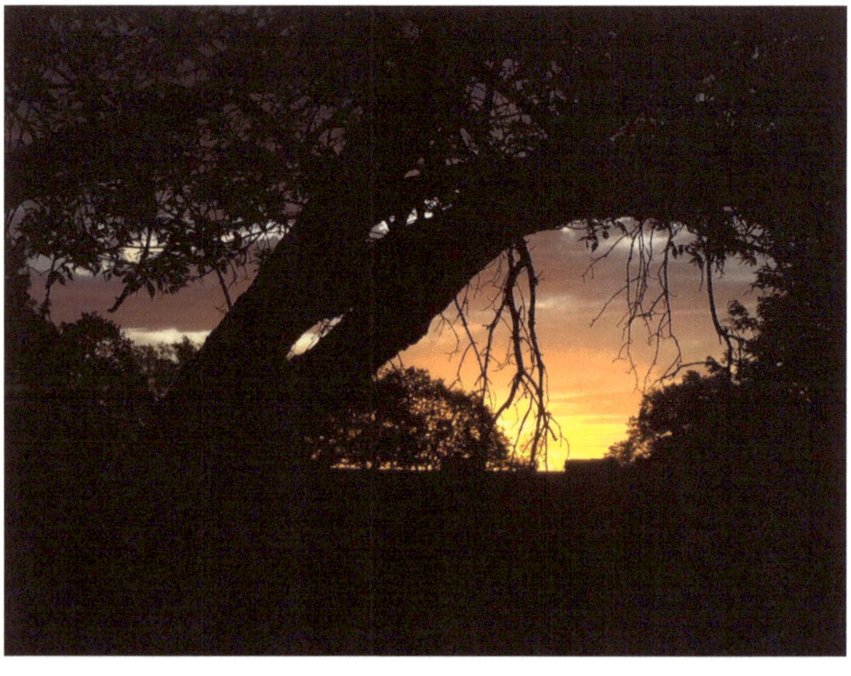

I will tell you when

Covid-19, when will you leave?

I will tell you when

When humanity's knees break and praying to God, who used to be the last thing becomes a necessity early each morning

When humanity remembers that, this world, to be enjoyed was solely created by God to be cared for by mankind

When humanity starts caring more about the people around them instead of always fixating on themselves

When humanity's thirst for money and possessions dies from lack of air and it starts wondering if there should have been a better way to live

When humanity's leaders realize that their positions of power were given to them by God and their decisions are required to be guided by Him

When God's will prevails

Until then...

May 7, 2020

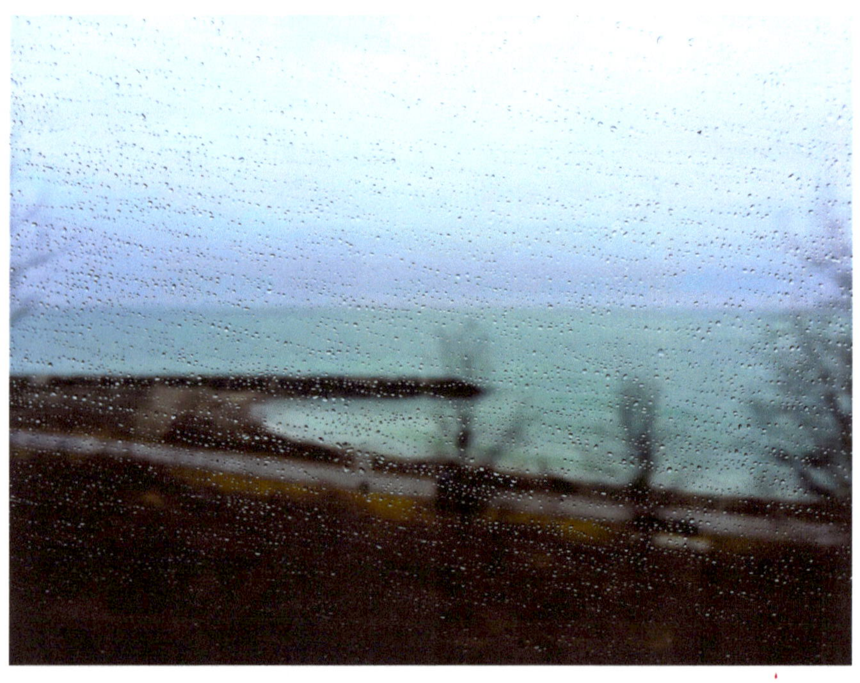

Through me

Sunday will be difficult...I know my friend
She left too soon, everyone we care about always do
We weren't created to say "Goodbye!"
The original plan did not include this parting of loved ones
This is when our faith kicks in

"Trust Me," says the Lord

And when we respond "Yes God, I trust You!"
Then God sends beautiful gifts:
Comfort, peace, reassurance, and love
And I hope these gifts will be given to you through me
Love you friend

Same as you welcomed me in your home and your heart
God has welcomed your mom to His home and His heart
She is safe, she is loved, she is always with you, and she is finally
home

May 8, 2020

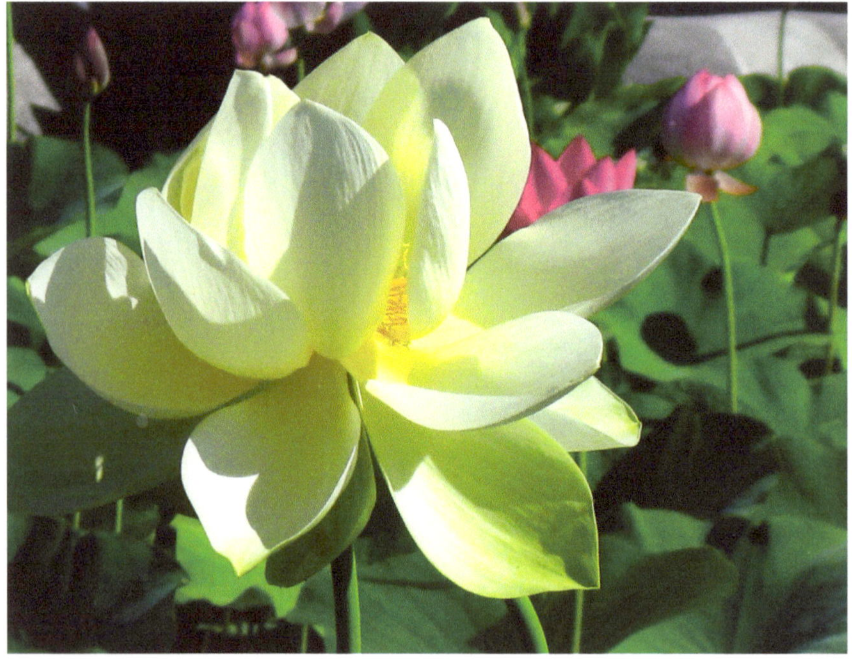

¡Feliz día mamá!

Una mamá

Elle est là pour te donner la vie, she's here to give you life
Elle est là pour te bercer, she's here to comfort you
Elle est là pour te tenir la main, she's here to hold your hand

Una mamá

Elle est là pour t'écouter, she's here to listen to you
Elle est là pour t'aider à grandir, she's here to help you grow
Elle est là pour t'encourager, she's here to encourage you

Una mamá

Elle est là pour essuyer tes larmes, she's here to dry your tears
Elle est là pour danser avec toi, she's here to dance with you
Elle est là pour te sourire, she's here to smile at you

Una mamá

Avant tout, elle est là pour t'aimer
Above all, she's here to love you

¡Feliz día maravillosa mamá!

May 9, 2020

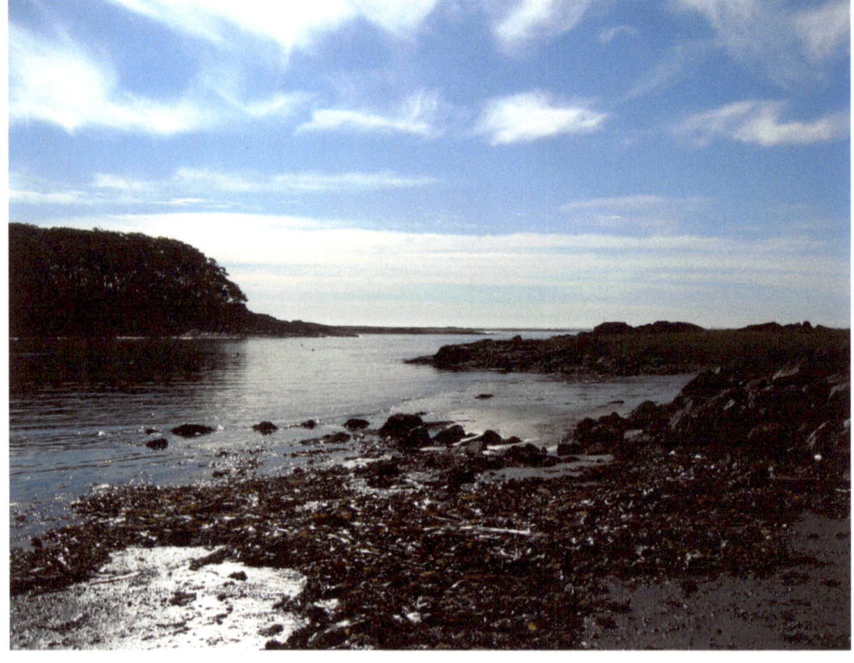

In the safe hand of God

My friend is struggling
Eyes heavy with tears

I don't know how to help
But I know Who can

My friend is kind and generous
Beautiful soul devoted to God

So I share a picture
A picture I see in my mind

The safe hand of God is closing so softly around you
Just enough so you don't fall

You are safe, loved, and at peace inside His hand
You can choose to look what is ahead
Or you may choose to hide your head

You feel His strength and He is getting you through this
difficult time
He is in motion, not you

The difficulty will not be avoided

But God is running head on and getting you to the other side
He is the one running, so just let Him

Anything you're still holding on
Just let it go
He will catch it
That is what He wants...

Trust Him with everything!

May 10, 2020

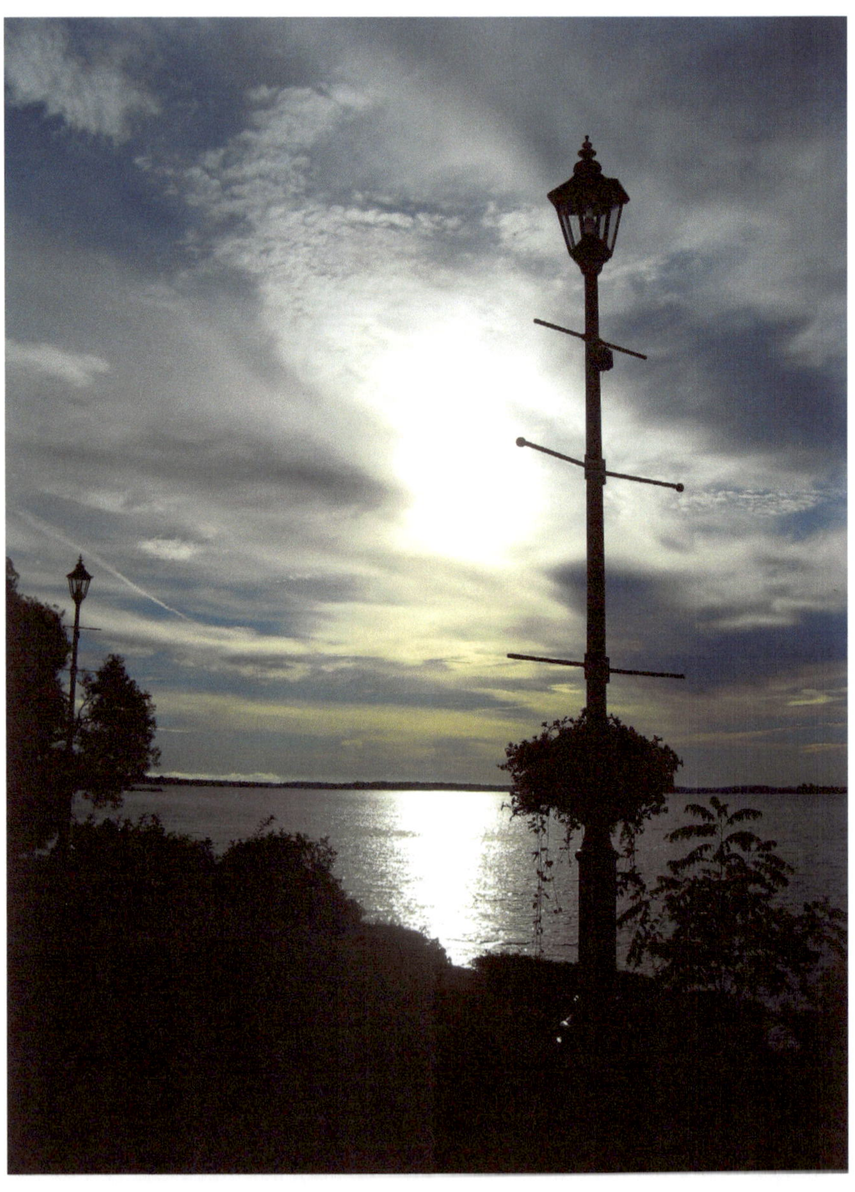

Feliz dia dos pais! ¡Feliz día del padre!

Quand je prie
Je prie à notre Père

When I pray
I pray to our Father

Les pères de la terre ont une grande responsabilité
Ils représentent, sur terre, notre Papa du ciel

The earthly fathers have an important role
They represent, here on Earth, our Heavenly Father

Ils sont forts, ils protègent
Ils aident, ils aiment

They are strong, they protect
They help, they love

Ils aiment la vie, ils donnent la vie

They love life, they give life

Ils consolent, ils écoutent
Ils guident, ils partagent

They comfort, they listen
They guide, they share

Tu représentes notre Papa sur terre et tu le fais bien mon ami !
You represent our Dad, here on Earth, and you do it well my
friend!

May 11, 2020

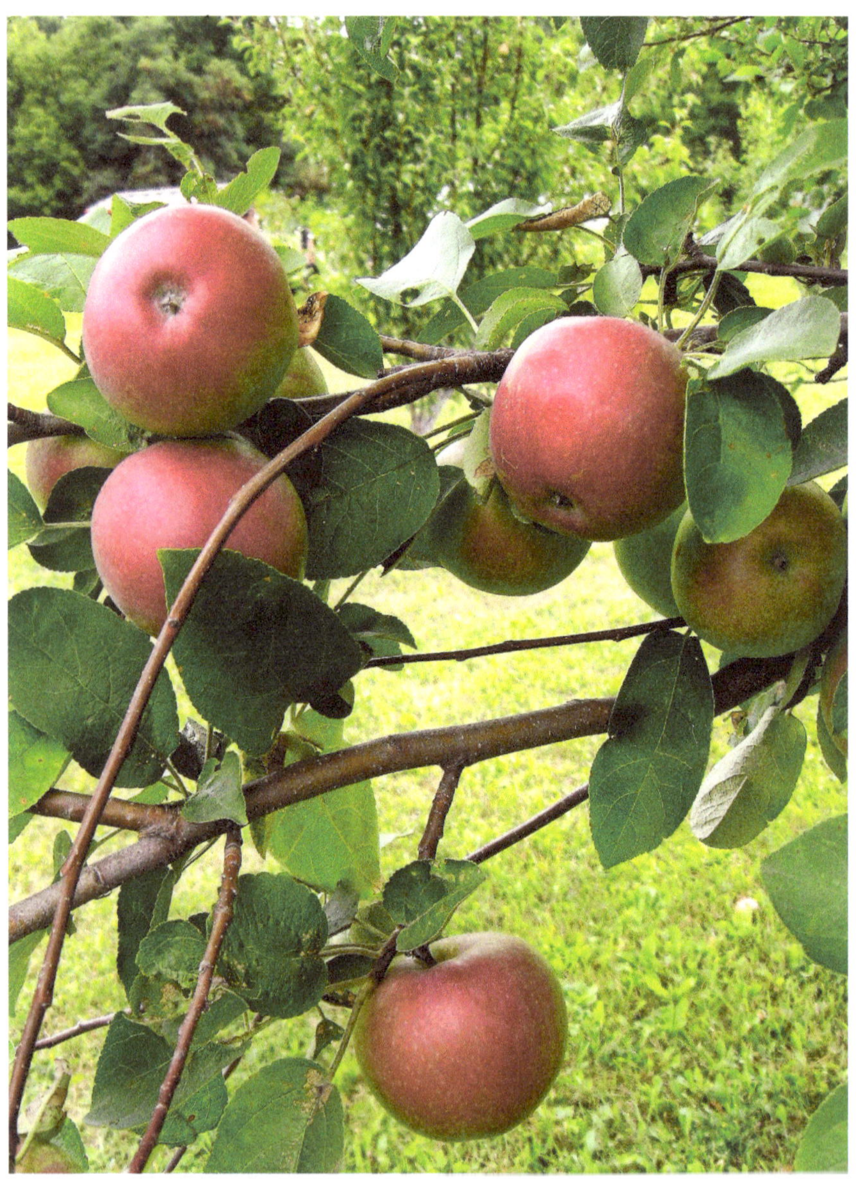

Give me a pure heart Father

Give me a pure heart Father
A heart that pleases You

Make it soft in Your hand
Make it respond to Your call

Show me all the rocks to be removed
So You may flow through me

Give me a pure heart Father
A heart that pleases You

Make it hear Your voice
Make it follow You

A harvest of good fruits, You promised
If we abide in You

That's what my heart wants
To be a heart that pleases You

May 12, 2020

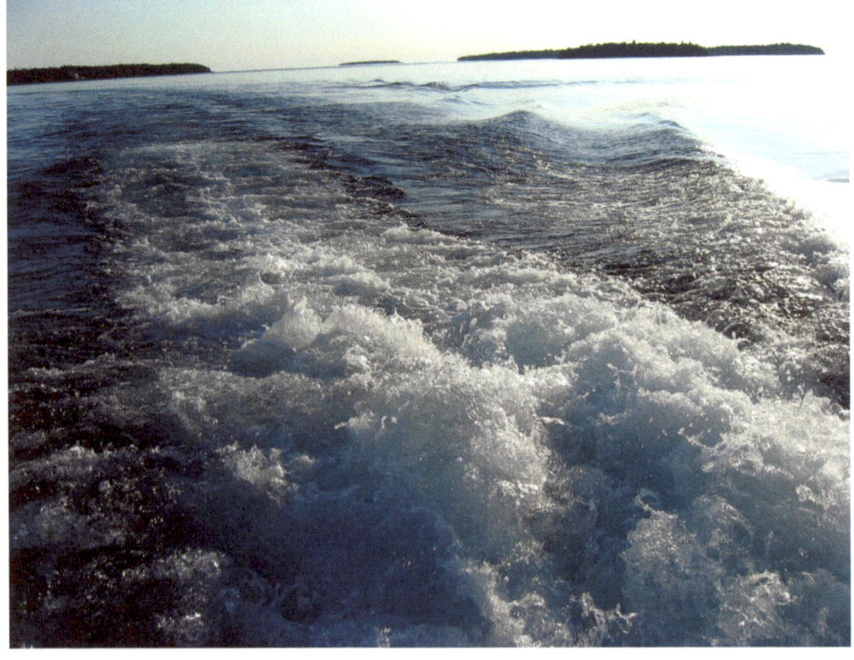

Everything belongs to You

Everything belongs to You

There are words that I organize
They change places in my mind

Once I'm happy
They are here for all to see

But they are not mine
Everything belongs to You

It's Your pen that scratches Your paper
It's Your ink that flows

It's Your ideas that birthed in my head
Your words that I rearrange

Something You guide me to read this morning
Triggered Your thought to wake up in my mind

So I pick up Your pen and I scratch Your paper
With the beauty that came to life inside my head

From Your hand to mine You flow through
Words You already had arranged

May 12, 2020

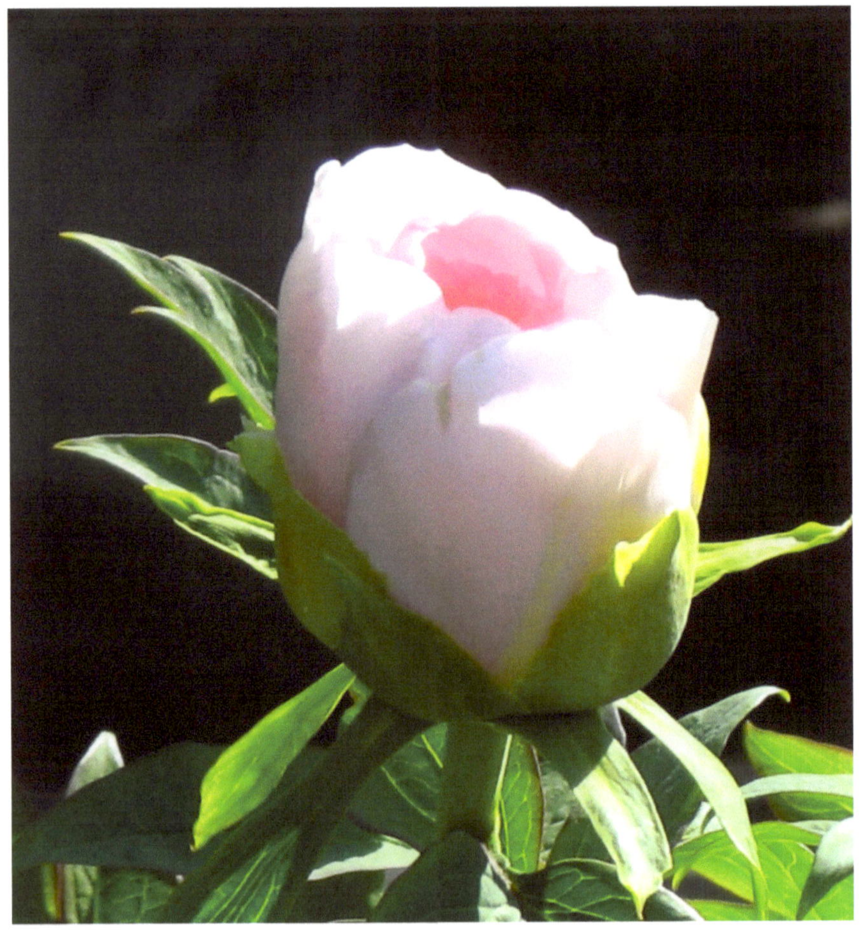

A spark

A spark
A spark exploded in your heart
A spark you didn't feel before

The size of a mustard's seed, said Jesus on a different subject

But is it really
A different subject?

When the spark that ignites is the spark of God's love
This tiny fire, full of God's power, will do more than move mountains

Love is an action word
Love is not passive; it compels you to take action

To serve
To give
To comfort

To help
To guide
To forgive

A spark is all a roaring fire needs
When it starts in a willing heart

A spark has ignited

A spark of God's love

May 13, 2020

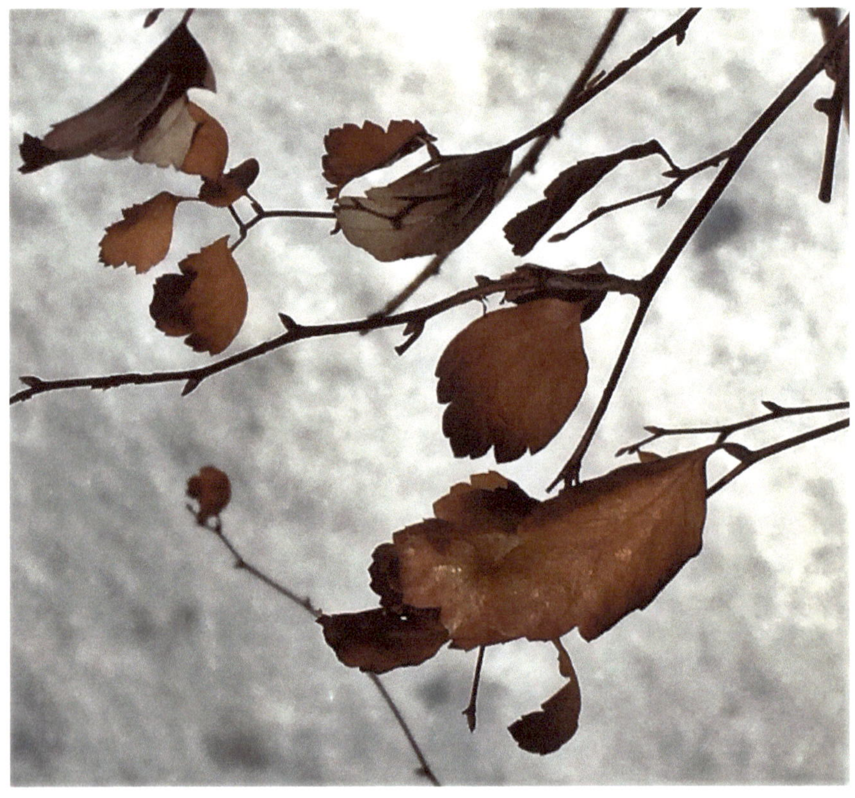

Two candles

Two candles close together
Shared the same fire

This joining made them stronger

Like a dance, the flame waved back and forth
With the wind of life

A time came when one of the candles broke in two and the
pieces melted

Only one candle remained
The light was no longer as bright

There was no joining and it felt a bit cold

Didn't want to dance anymore
With the wind of life

A time came when the flame got stronger again
The candle was close to the ground by then

The short wick finally reached the fallen one and the dancing
started again

May 15, 2020

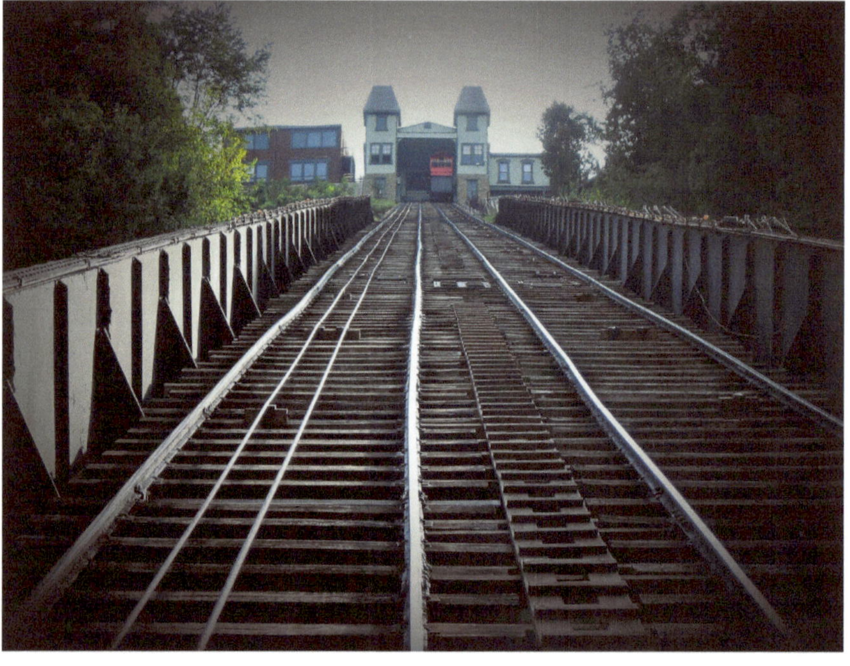

All aboard!

Oh! The joy of planning a vacation
We know where we're going
How long we're going to stay
What we'll do once we get there
And we know how many days
Till departure day

I'm not really in the mood these days
To travel anywhere
Not with this ugly red spiky thing loose in our cities

But there is a trip I don't want to miss
So I got my ticket
I got it many years ago

It will be the longest trip I ever took
It's actually a one-way ticket

I'm leaving on H day

Heaven

Oh! I read books about it
No words we know can accurately describe it
The beauty, the brightness
Even some colours don't exist here on Earth

Oh! And the love
It is like nothing we ever felt before
Once you get there you never want to leave
What a wonderful place!

I'll go there one day
Anyone can, it's so simple

You don't need to pack anything
You don't make an itinerary
You don't know when you leave
But you know how long you'll stay

Well, what kind of trip is that? You say
What kind of travel agency can stay in business offering trips
like these?
You don't know much about your destination
You don't know when you leave, and what is this thing about
 not bringing anything?

Oh don't concern yourself with earthly things! I say
This Travel Agency has been in business for thousands of years
The Travel Agent is a friend of mine
His Father owns Heaven
His Father is also mine

I got my ticket many years ago
I agree, the departure date and time are hidden from me
It's best this way

Like all organized trips, the Travel Agent provided all the
information needed
To take that trip
I hope you decide to get your ticket too

Don't be afraid of the day, nor the time of your departure
The Travel Agent will be there with you
He promised and He never lies

Oh! I love surprises
One day I'll hear
All aboard!
Such beautiful words that open Heaven for me

Get your ticket and you will hear it too

May 17, 2020

We pray with You

Jesus, You said: "If two of you agree here on Earth concerning anything you ask, my Father in Heaven will do it for you. For where two or three gather together in My name, I am there among them."

We are two or three gathered together in Your name, so You are here among us

Speak to us
We're here to listen

Make us see
Our hearts are open

Make us hear what You're saying
Make us grow
Make us trust You with everything

"Pandemic is not new to this world." You say
"It's just new to you."

God allowed it, at this point in time, to get our attention, and it worked
But mostly to teach us something
And this is where it's not working
Lots of people are not listening to You
Too many don't spend any time with You
You knock at the door, but they don't answer
You are patient so You wait for them and You pray

Our prayers are joining Yours
We pray with You, Jesus

We pray for all that don't listen to You
We pray for all whose hearts are not open to You
We pray for all that refuses to trust You
We pray for all who choose other gods besides You

We pray for all who don't care to have a relationship with You
We pray for all who can't see what a Life is with You
We pray for all that hear You on the other side, yet they don't
answer You

We pray with You that they open the door and welcome You

May 19, 2020

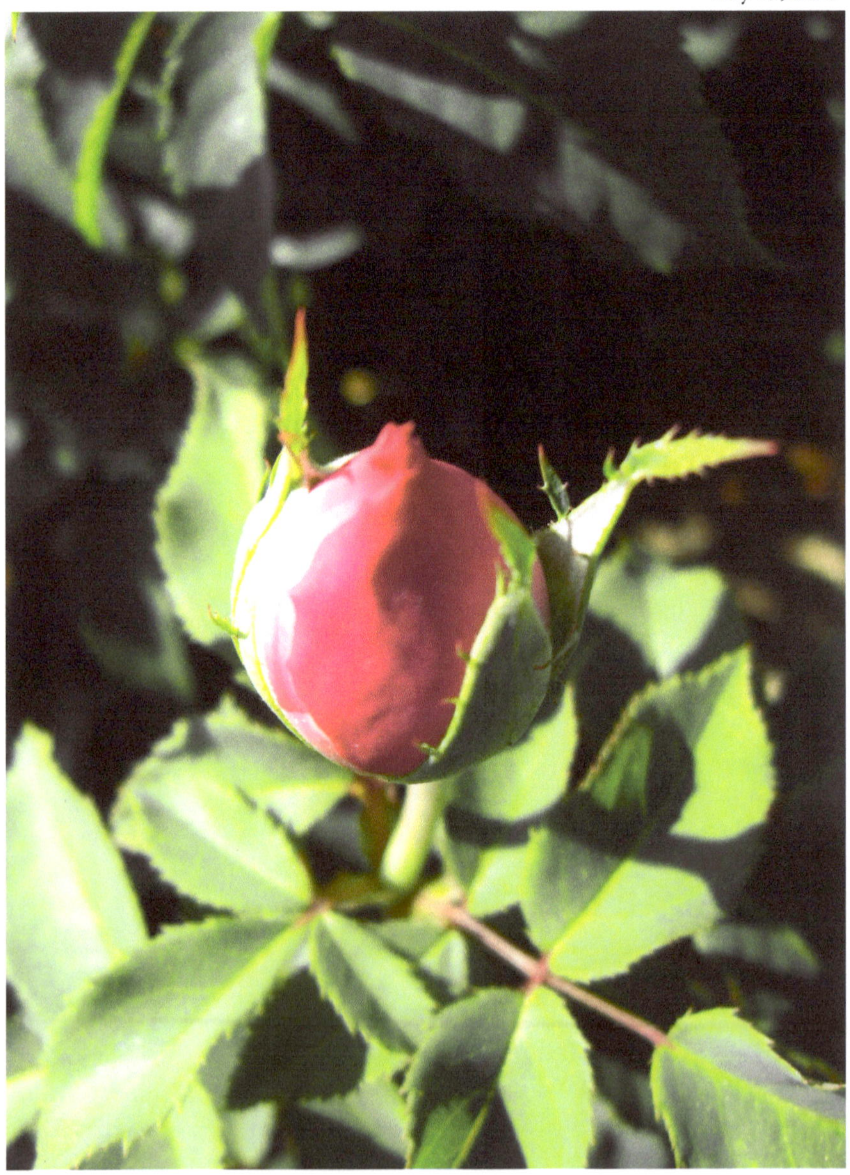

There is a shadow

A shadow cannot exist in total darkness
It needs light and an object
And when the object gets illuminated, a shadow is born

There is a shadow in Psalm 23
A shadow because of Your Light
Jesus, when You shine on us, a shadow is born

Death still exists, the valley is still there
But because of Your Light, the darkness took a step back
And we see the shadow

When we walk
We know You're here because of it
And Your presence kills our fear

Soon we will see the valley disappear
There will be time before another one
But all along, the shadow never dies
Because You walk with us
Your Light never stops shining on us
And the shadow never dies

May 20, 2020

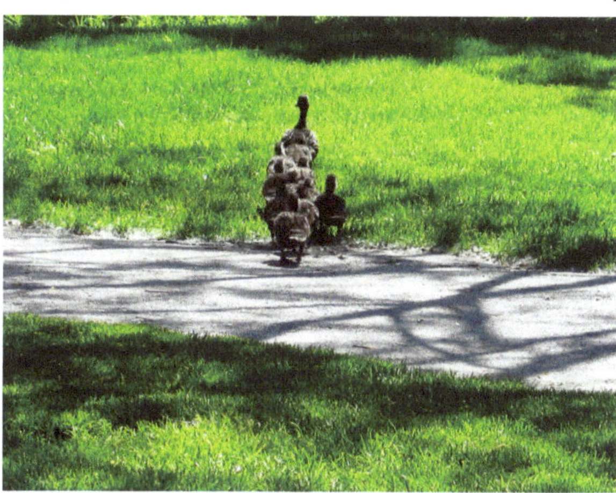

Seasons

I remember a spring
So many years ago
A short time
A gift from God
Like all seasons, it faded to make room for the next one

But what if, instead of fading to nothing, something had
remained
Something I was fond of in that season that would twist itself
around the next one
The twirling could repeat itself with each season, so it would
always remain with me

Oh I know what I would have kept!

I loved the smell of the air that spring
Something fresh, sweet, and exhilarating was in it
It never came back again
It was only that year
I wish it would still be twirling

I wonder if it came from Heaven
A little door that was left open
Someone in the sky had forgotten to close it properly

God saw it and smiled
And decided to give it to me each day that spring
He blew gently in my direction through the door
So the breeze would catch me down here

When the season was ending
God slowly closed it back again
Back for good this time

There are also these friends that God gave me at different
seasons
That journeyed with me a short time
I wish they would still be twirling
I miss them
I miss spending time with them
They had to take a different road than mine
They had to take a different path in life

But since all journeys...well
All journeys, for God's children that is
Lead to Him
The end of our journeys will reunite us

I hope to hear when I see them
"Oh how I have missed you!
Oh how I have missed spending time with you!"

And with Heaven's perfume twirling around us
I'll answer, "Me too, oh so much!"

May 22, 2020

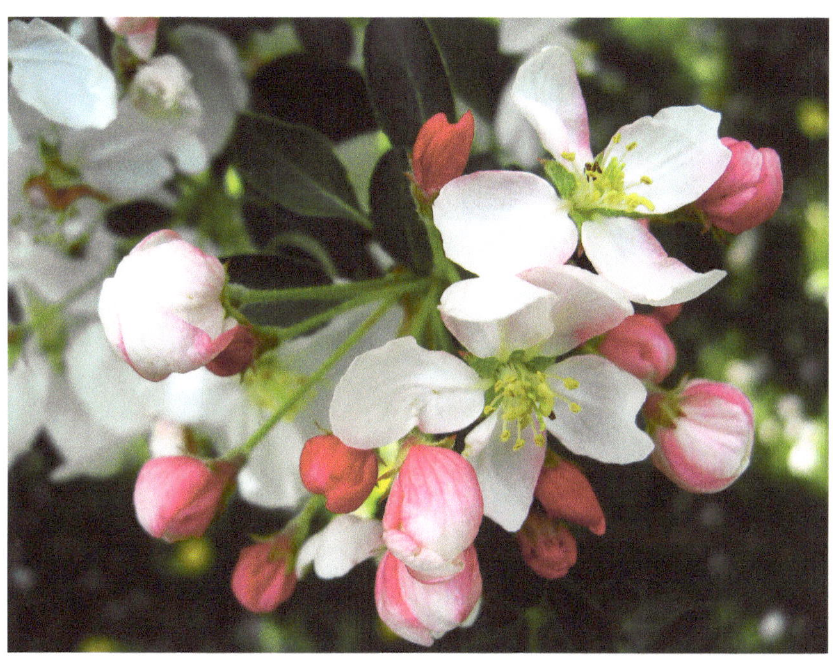

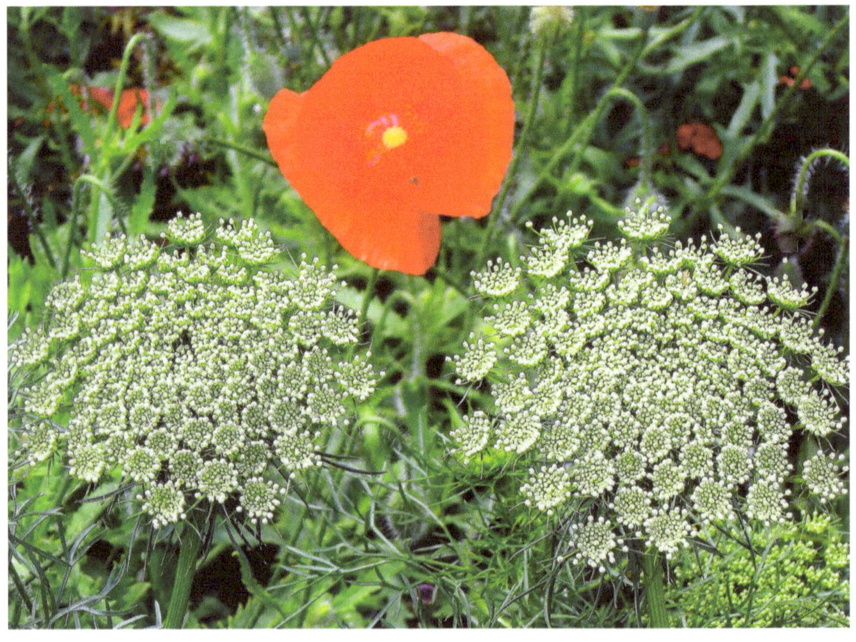

A French flower

The little rabbit woke up very early
His nose started to twitch
The aroma had awakened him, something was new

Being curious, even just before the dawn
He peeked outside and saw
That it looked safe to come out

He hopped a few yards
His nose guiding him
And then he saw

A red flower, a poppy
She was stretching her petals
And perfume was escaping

The sweet scent was intoxicating
The little rabbit was mesmerized
With glazed eyes, he lost his heart and fell in love

She saw him and smiled
« Bonjour ! » She said
"I'm Coquelicot. Is this your garden?"

"Hi! No...well...maybe it is...I'm the only rabbit here, so maybe
it is."
He answered back puffing his chest but then he started to
blush because she was quite pretty

"Would you like a tour?" he asked
"I can't, you see, I'm bound to my stem."
"Can't you detach yourself, just for a little while?"
"Well, I don't know, I never tried before, I just bloomed a few
minutes ago."

So, she bent her stem and he scooped her up
And together he showed her his garden

The pond with its lilies
The tall grass and the hill
A sleeping piglet next to some deer

She saw all the colours
And the flowers between the trees

"I'm thirsty," she said
So, the flower returned to her stem

"Will you come back?" she asked
"Yes," he answered

The next morning, when she woke up
He had a surprise for her
During the night, he had made himself a new home
At the bottom of her stem

"After all," he said
"Aroma is everything!"

She smiled and he kissed her
Because, you see, she had fallen, also
In love, that is!

May 23, 2020

Different that way

Funny thing that
Before Covid-19
Lots of people didn't have time to spend with friends
I mean, face to face
A text, an email was the only thing given to them
A phone call, oh but only rarely!

"Who has time for face to face?" I heard them say

I sort of always prefer that with dear friends
But then again, I was different that way

Was I the only one?

Funny thing that
Now with Covid-19
People are no longer satisfied with a text, an email or even a
phone call

All of a sudden, with this isolation
They crave the face to face I adore
They noticed that video chat is a poor substitute for what they
desire now

Funny thing that
They want what was available in abundance before Covid-19
But then they didn't

There were plenty of face-to-face opportunities before
But they choose to do something else

"Who has the time?" they kept saying

Was I the only one?

Do you crave it now because you have too much time?

I wonder
And I hope not

After Covid-19
What will you do?
Go back to a text, an email or rarely a phone call
Or will you...then...be like me, different that way

May 23, 2020

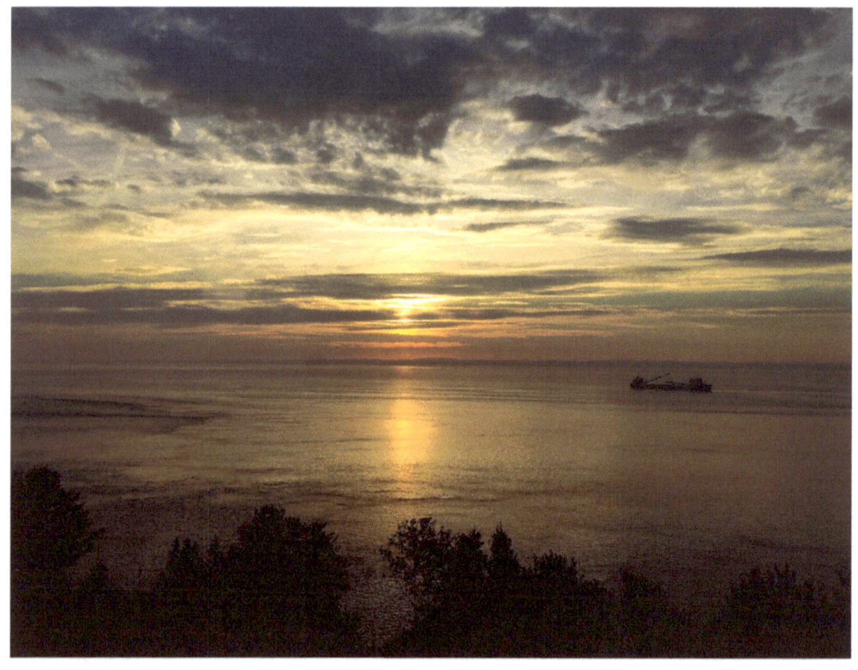

Walk towards the Light

You see many roads
You don't know where to go

In the distance you see a very faint Light
So you head in that direction

"Walk towards the Light,"
You hear in your soul

There are boulders and pebbles on the road
"Is this really the way?" you ask yourself

And you hear it again in your soul
"Walk towards the Light."

So you climb over the boulders
And you sink slightly among the pebbles
There is some grass up ahead
To refresh your journey

Now the road is full of sunshine
You're walking next to some water
The sand under your feet is soft and warm
It's beautiful

All of a sudden
It gets really dark
A mountain size boulder
Just crashed and blocked the road

But this time
Your faith is stronger

You don't ask yourself

"Is this really the way?"

You rock climb your mountain through Christ
And you remember another verse

Draw near to God and He will draw near to you
How joyful you are that you did

Walk towards the Light

May 24, 2020

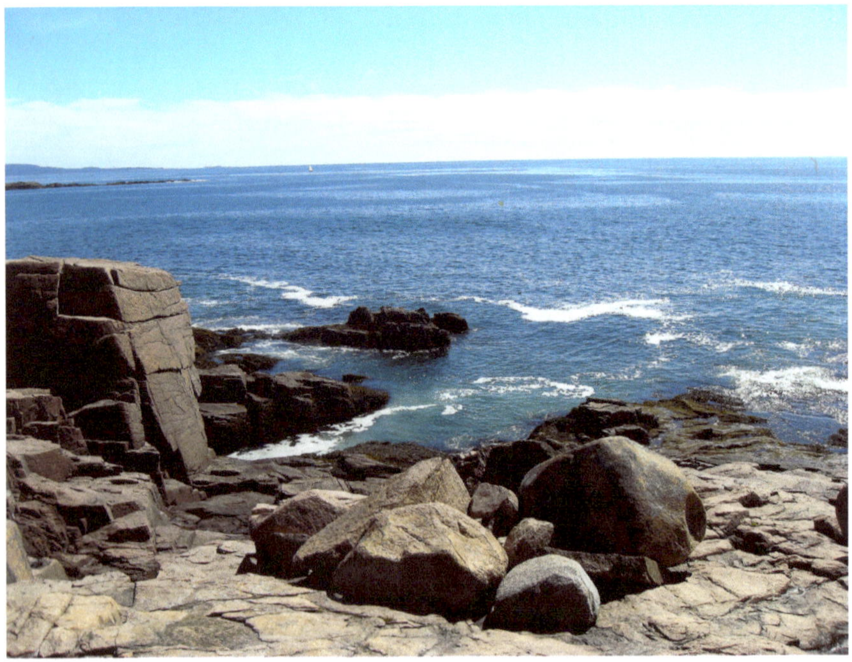

Go where God guides you instead

Don't be lured by the praises of others
They may not have your best interest at heart
They may want to direct your steps, for what's best for them

Go to God and put your trust in Him
Ask for guidance and listen; let Him show you the way

He knows which people you are to meet
And all the tests you'll need to pass along the way

He crafted your journey

God knows which steps to take
He envisioned it all with your best interest at heart

Your gifts and talents were given to you
By God, for His Glory
You are meant to use them for Him

He will place you where He wants you to shine
You may not see the darkness of this place, but God does
So shine, as brightly as you can

Your gifts and talents are perfect for this place
The place He chose for you

Someone here needs to hear
What God will prompt you to say

Someone needs your caring
Someone needs your boldness
Someone needs your gentle whisper

Don't deny them, they are hurting, and they need you

And as far as praises are concerned
Don't go where people lure you to go
Go where God guides you instead
The joy you will have there doesn't compare

May 26, 2020

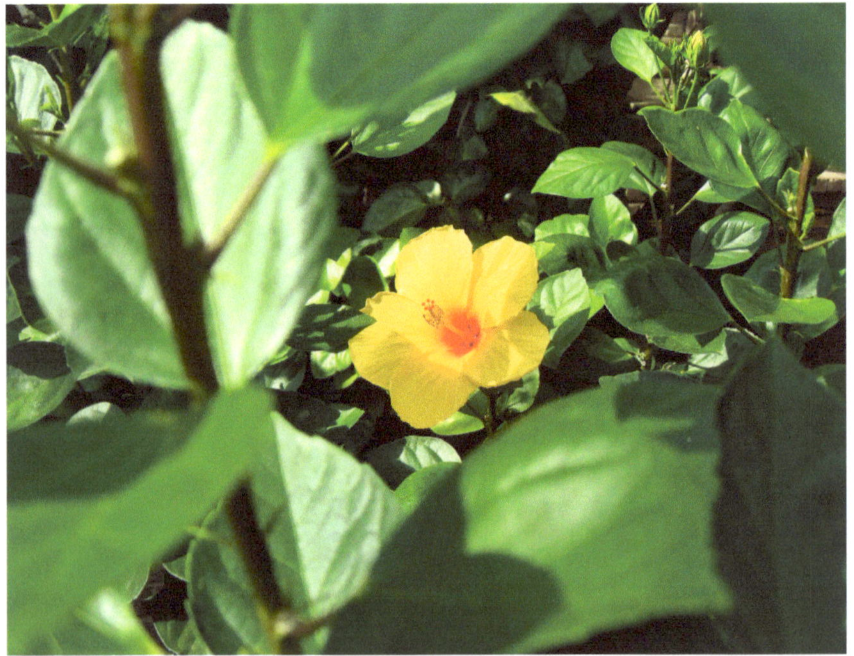

Keep and give

There is a powerful principle that comes from God
A key, a secret I am sharing with you
Keep and give

Keep a smile for yourself
Give one to someone who would like one

Keep some bread for yourself
Give some bread to someone who needs some

Keep some of your kindness towards yourself
Give the rest to someone else

Keep encouraging yourself
Give encouragement to those who have fallen and need some

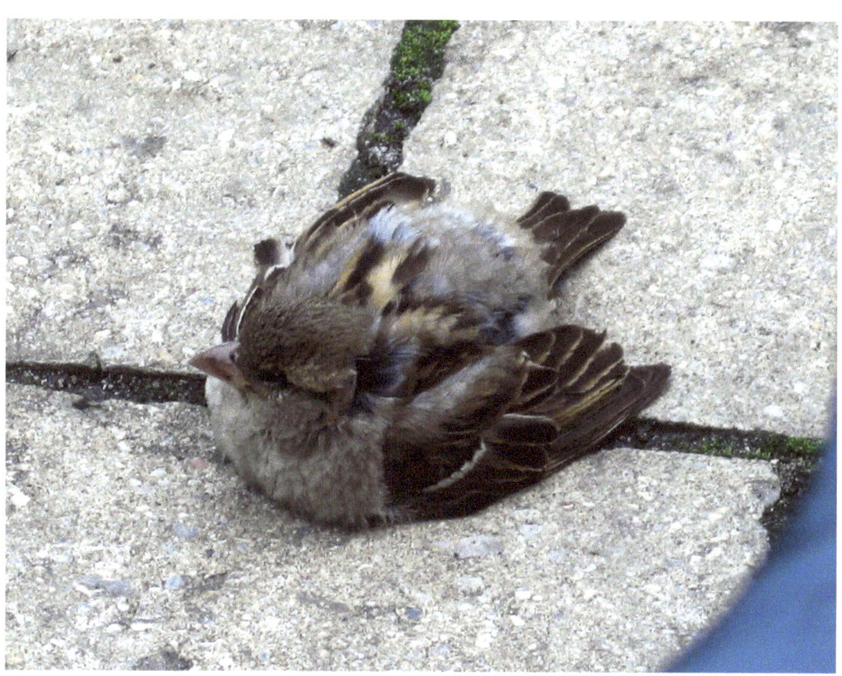

Keep and save some of God's given resources for your needs
Give generously the remaining

Keep accepting God's forgiveness when you ask Him
Give forgiveness to others to lighten their burdens

There are other principles
With action words different from keep and give
They do share the same secret for joy in life

Love the person God made in you
Love others as yourself

Be loyal to God
Be a loyal friend to someone

Be honest with God and yourself
Be honest with others

Celebrate God
Celebrate yourself
Celebrate with others
Celebrate others

May 27, 2020

The yellow caterpillar and the tiny mouse

A yellow caterpillar had a sister and two brothers. Came a day when they all changed to butterflies except for him. He wasn't sure why but that didn't bother him.

Each day he would go slowly up the ridge, eating his lunch along the way. At the top, he would tuck in all his million legs and he would roll down, laughing. He was a happy yellow caterpillar.

One day, when he had gone halfway up, he saw a tiny mouse just sitting there. She looked very sad, so he interrupted his lunch to found out why.

"I don't know where my friend is. He was no longer home when I woke up this morning."

"I can be your friend, if you want," he replied.

"I would like that very much." She smiled back. "I'm very fond of caterpillar," she said. "They make the best of friends, they are fluffy and soft, and at night they like to wrap themselves around me to help me fall asleep. I get frightened easily, because I'm a tiny mouse. This morning I woke up and it had happened again, my caterpillar friend was gone. I don't know where he went, and I'm frightened again."

"Don't worry, tiny mouse, I'll be your friend. I'm lonely too; my sister and my brothers are gone. Come, follow me up the ridge, I'll show you a game."

After a few steps, the tiny mouse had an idea. "Climb onto my back." So, he did, and soon she was zooming up with him up the ridge.

Once they got to the top, he showed her how to tuck her tiny legs in so she could roll down with him, laughing.

They played that game many times. Usually it would take him all day just to go down one time.

It got darker and the tiny mouse became nervous. "Let's go home," she said. They did and he made sure she was all tucked in before he fell asleep that night.

The next morning, when they were slowly eating breakfast, a nasty peacock came, flaunting his colourful feathers.

"Well, well, well, what do we got here, you found yourself another squirmy worm I see. Haven't you learned your lesson by now, tiny mouse?"

She didn't answer and soon the peacock went away.

"He's a very beautiful bird," she said.

"Not inside," answered the yellow caterpillar.

The tiny mouse stopped eating, looked at her new friend and realized he was right.

"I like you," she smiled. "Do you know everything?"

"Probably not," he smiled back. "But I can tell when someone is only beautiful outside."

"The peacock is wrong," she said. "You are beautiful inside and outside."

Then it was his turn to stop eating and look at her. Then he smiled and said: "I like you. Do you know everything?" Repeating her words and the tiny mouse giggled.

A few days later, when she woke up, a beautiful butterfly had wrapped itself around her.

"Who are you? Where's my friend?" She was getting frightened again.

He smiled back. "Don't worry, it's me."

"Oh! What happened to you, you look different?"

"That's what a caterpillar does. After a certain time, we all change to butterflies."

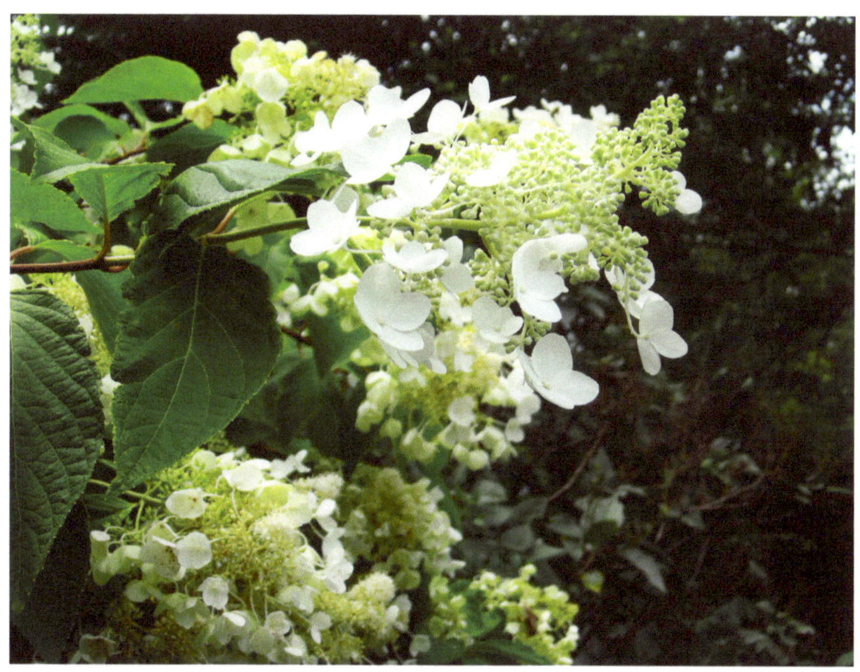

"Oh, so that's what happened to all my friends. That's why all the butterflies around here always come to say hi, and I didn't know why so I kept running away because I'm a tiny mouse and I was frightened. They were all my old friends; I didn't have to be afraid. Will you leave also, then?" she sadly asked.

"Oh no, come, let's go play that game," he replied.

This time, the yellow butterfly picked her up and they flew up the ridge and she made sure she waved hello to all the fluttering butterflies they encounter along the way.

"Come play with us," she said.

And since then, a tiny mouse with her legs tucked in is seen rolling down laughing with her zillions of friends, colourful butterflies with their wings tucked in.

May 27, 2020

The cherry tree

Close to a lake
With lush grass at its feet
Lives a cherry tree

It had learned over the years
That its job was subject to change
After a few months, came a different role

Summer is for producing fruits
Lots of them to feed the birds
Create sweets, desserts, and red jam

Autumn is when the tree starts to rest
The branches explode in many colours
The green gives its place to gold and different shades of orange
and red

Winter brings cold, snow, and ice that is seen on the lake
The tree retrieves its sap, and hibernation starts for a well-
deserved rest
The leaves, suddenly free, enrol for flying lessons with the wind

Spring gives the signal for the leaves to start growing again
It also brings white and pink flowers blooming on every
branch
Petals cover the grass around the tree like a delicate veil

Then it's summer again with its long days
And the tree provides shade from the heat
To all that come close to him to rest

And all are welcome to eat a handful of red cherries

May 28, 2020

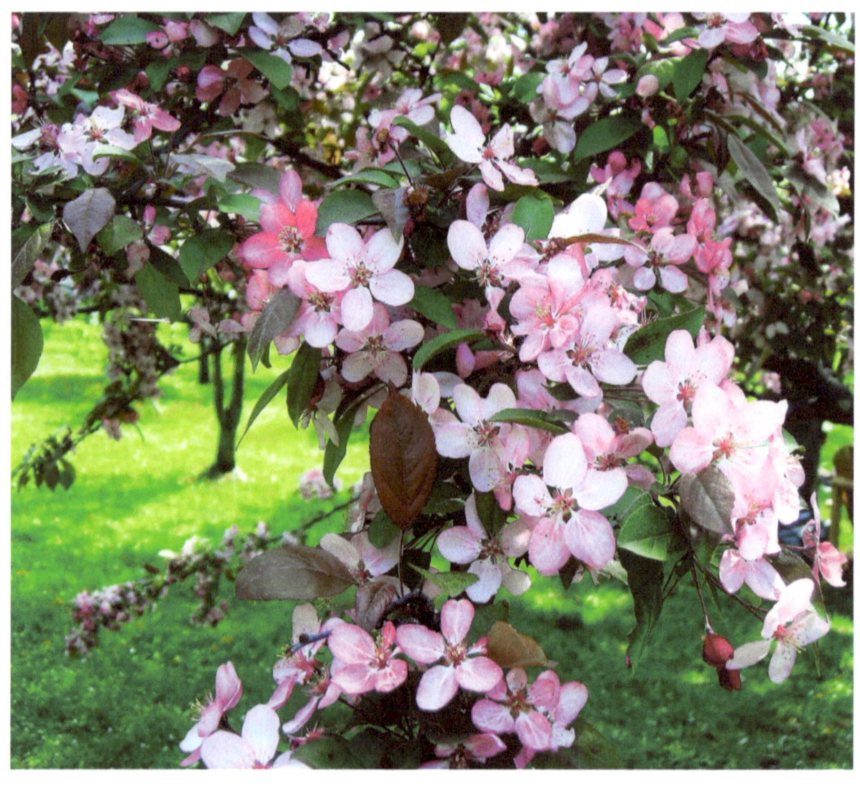

Teddy

Teddy had only one goal today
Take a nap on the floor near the blue tile

Yesterday, while she was being dragged
She noticed the spot

As long as no one moves the curtain
The sun's rays should fall just right

She had a number of obstacles to deal with before the nap

For one thing, her means of transportation were limited
Her legs were not very strong and then, there was that dog

She was sharing the toddler's love with a sloppy one

Teddy was not too fond when he was throwing her around just
for fun
He already chewed her tail off
And now, standing was another issue, no balance
What a shame for a cat!

But Teddy hasn't seen the dog today
If he's hiding, that means, today's Tuesday

Laundry day, bath day
Oh, it's perfect!

After that, in the dryer, Teddy would hold on to the blanket
And when mom would put away the clothes and the rest
She was going to let go and drop to the floor and bounce right
next to the blue tile

Soon, the sleepy stuffed teddy bear was drifting slowly to sleep
bathing in the sun

She wondered why the toddler kept calling her Teddy
What a weird name for a cat

True, she could not feel any whiskers
Her ears were not very pointy
They were actually quite round

And just before she fell asleep
She finally understood why
She was all brown with no stripes

"Now why did I think I was a cat?"
She yawned and drifted off to sleep

May 28, 2020

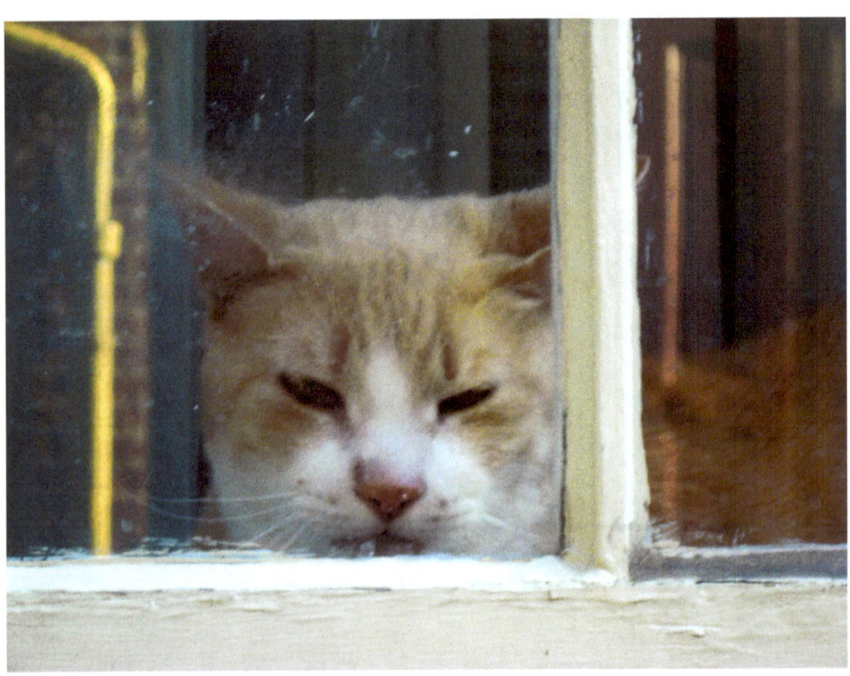

Power in life

Difficult moments are part of life
I have them like everyone else

Times when you feel kind of dead inside from too much grief

Someone you love has passed on or
Something is crushing your heart or
You have to take a difficult route or face something you would
rather not

I remember the first time I dealt with these types of moments
When simply being or breathing is difficult
I remember being surprised that outside
Life just went on

How come?

How can the sun just simply rise as if nothing has happened?
How can the Earth continue to turn?
How can people just go on to work like a normal day?
There is nothing normal about today

How come life just went on when mine felt like it stopped that
day?

There is power in life
You can see that power even in small things

Grass can find a crack in concrete and grow there
A ladybug can fall on its back and will struggle tremendously
until she is right side up again

I remember as a kid, in my neighbourhood, there was a white
dog

A gorgeous long white-haired husky
I didn't like dogs back then because I was afraid of them
But that dog; Oh! I was always happy to see him

He was calm and he loved children
I was never scared of him; I remember stroking his fur
A nice moment of friendship

That beautiful dog had three legs, something had happened of
course
I can still see him in my mind, happy as can be, he just walked
differently
I'm sure he had no clue that dogs came with four
Or he did but he didn't care

It left a strong impression on me, a hope
He had found a way to go on and be happy again

And when the pain is not as fresh
Seeing that life does go on
Helps us do the same thing

It stirs up something inside
That power that is in life
That power that will make us get up, continue living, and be
happy again

May 31, 2020

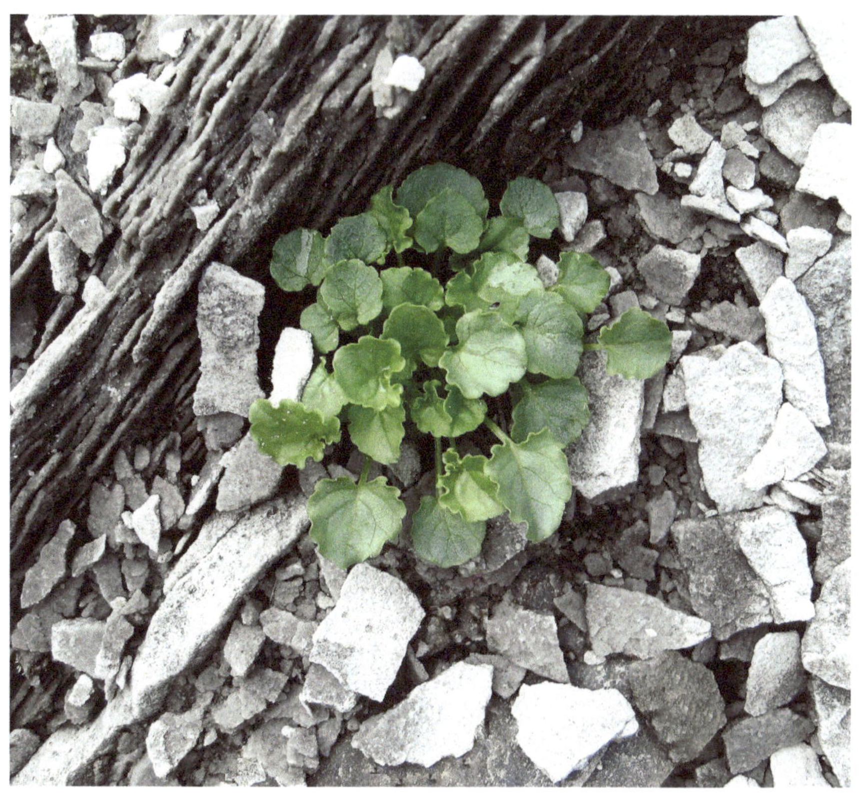

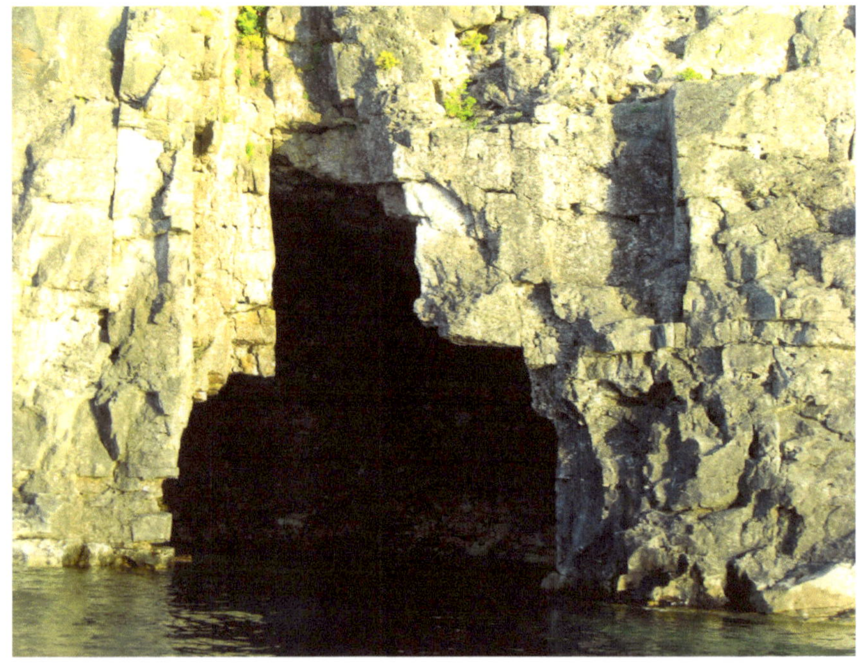

A life with You, now and for eternity

At age 33, You died for us
To pay for mankind's sin

If I close my eyes
I can see You
Barely able to walk
Your body all bruised
You are almost on the ground from the weight of the cross

The cross You are to carry to Your death

My heart breaks to see You like that
And I am so powerless to do anything to stop it
Even if I had lived back then
You would have stopped me if I had tried
Because there was no other way

Each Good Friday is a difficult day
We honour You, the magnitude of Your gift, the magnitude of
Your love
And our hearts feel Your death
But we know Sunday is coming
So we bear Friday because of Sunday, Your resurrection

You are no longer walking with that cross
Your body is no longer bruised
You're no longer dead

We embrace You
We embrace Easter Sunday
We embrace the gift given to us

Salvation

We are to tell all who don't know You
All those You prepare to hear

Who You are
What You did
What is offered to all

A life with You, now and for eternity

June 2, 2020

And it needs it now

I like taking photographs of flowers
Lilacs and tulips
Roses and carnations
Big bushes of peonies

The fact that flowers come in a multitude of different colours
doesn't bother anyone

And yet, just four different colours
When it comes to human skin...

I like to go to botanical gardens
They arrange such beautiful flowers beds
Mixing different kinds in a variety of colours

I have never heard anyone say: "I don't like blue flowers." for
instance
And then proceed to remove and tear up all the blue flowers
from gardens all over the world

And yet, just four different colours
When it comes to human skin...

Then we have all these artists
They revolve around colours, the more choices they have, the
more magnificent are the pieces they create
I don't need to continue
You know the rest

Our entire world overflows with amazing, gorgeous colours
Birds, trees, animals, beaches, sceneries, landscapes,
mountains...
And yet, just four...

Like everyone, I want a vaccine that kills Covid-19
So no more people get ill because of it
So no more people die because of it

But it is so far from being the only thing I want

The world needs a vaccine to eradicate
Racism, hatred, war, shooting, rampage, rage...
And it needs it now

June 2, 2020

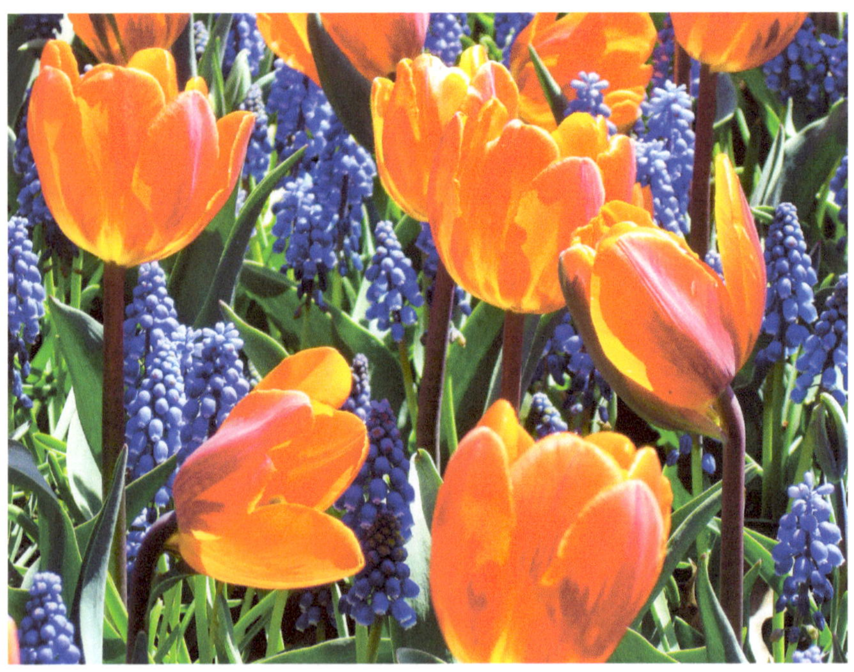

The boy with the red kite

The boy loves the beach
Early each sunny day
You can see him running near the shore
With his red kite

When he is satisfied it flies high enough
The boy lies on the sand
And just looks at his red kite
Flying in the sky

One morning
A pelican showed up
And sat near the boy
Looking, like him, at the red kite flying in the sky

The pelican came back each morning
So the boy started going to the beach, not only with his red
kite, but also a small fish for his new friend

They would sit together once the kite was in the air
A little closer each day

One morning, the pelican had a surprise for the boy
He ate the fish, spread his wings and took off

On his way up he grabbed the string in his beak
And flew higher and higher

He made the kite waltz near the ocean waves
Then moved it like a roller coaster high in the sky

The boy watched his red kite in amazement
And the show, his new friend, was putting on, just for him

Then the pelican returned the kite
And sat once again on the sand near the boy

He slowly tilted his head like the artist he was
Accepting the applause of his public; his friend
The boy with the red kite

June 2, 2020

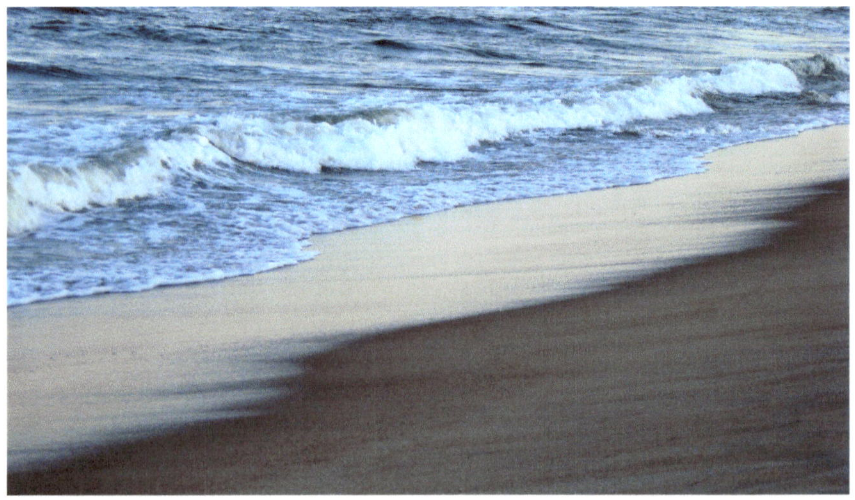

Nine words away

Prayer opens the door
For God to work in our lives

Prayer is to be our first
Response to everything

When you start your day
Give Him your first words
Give Him your first moment

A simple "Good morning Father; Thank You!"
An acknowledgment of His presence
Who He is from our grateful heart

Then, when problems come
"God, please help me, please help us, thank You!"
Just nine words, to open the door for God to help

Prayer is the first thing we are to do, always
Our first defence, our call for help, our grateful heart, our first
moment
Not the last one when everything else has failed

God's help is just nine words away

God is always ready to help

Open the door

It's just nine words away

Why stay alone struggling without God's help

I have seen with my own eyes His problem-solving skills

Skills that made me forget to breathe the first time
I saw what He did after I had said those nine words

Don't stay
Nine words away
Say them and see God's good powerful earth-shattering help

June 3, 2020

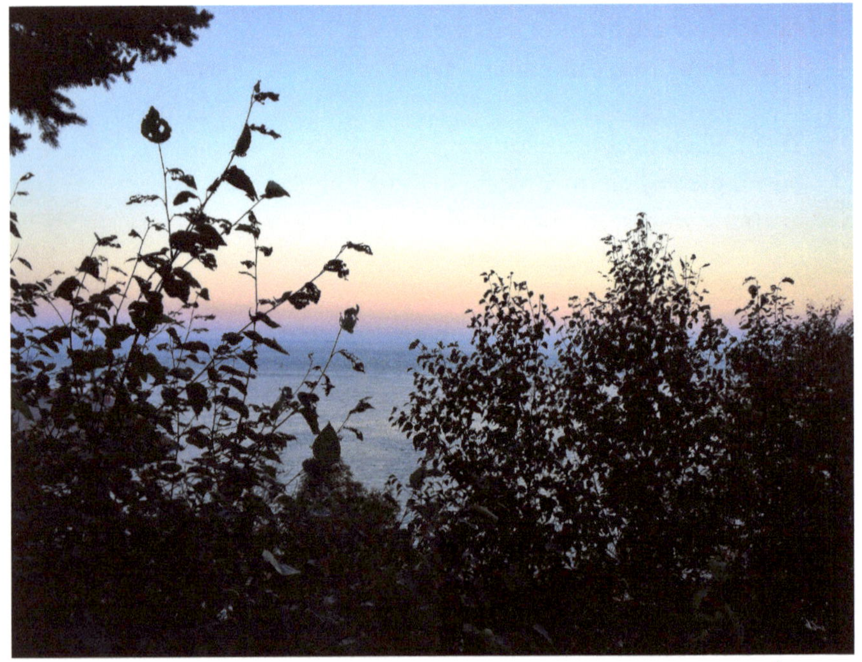

Something had begun

Like most people
When Covid-19 erupted in our lives
I stayed home and followed the rules to reduce the spread

But when your life revolves around helping others
I felt lost
Not knowing what to do

I prayed to God
Wondering what He wanted
What was I supposed to do now?

It didn't dawn on me back then
It does now
I was supposed to wait

It was a time when
Instead of being an acting participant
I was meant to wait and be patient

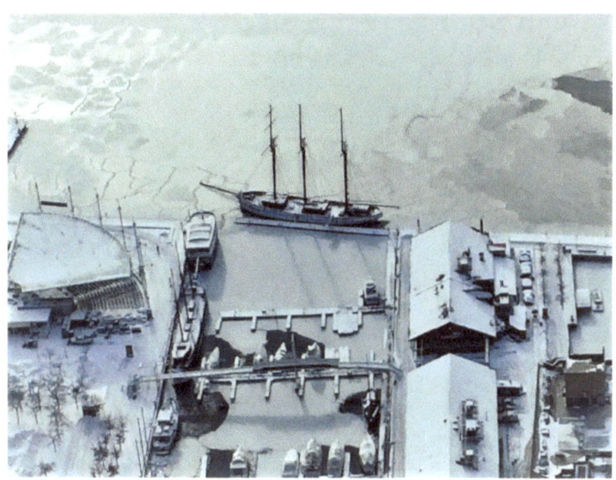

A time was coming, but not yet
I didn't foresee it then, but now I know better
God was working as always
He was going to create something beautiful

On April 19, something broke inside of me
I had had enough of that thing
That evil thing that was destroying life and I wanted some
happiness back

On April 20, something rose inside of me
I put on music, a particular piece I had recently heard,
something upbeat
I started to dance, fighting for part of what I had lost
I was so angry that day

Then an image came in my mind
And I could almost hear in that music, metal from marching
armor and heavy coordinated loud steps from army boots

I stopped
I grabbed a pen and poured all my anger on paper, something I
had never done before
This is how "I will again..." was born

I remember reading it a few times afterward
Stunned
Something had begun
Something beautiful

June 3, 2020

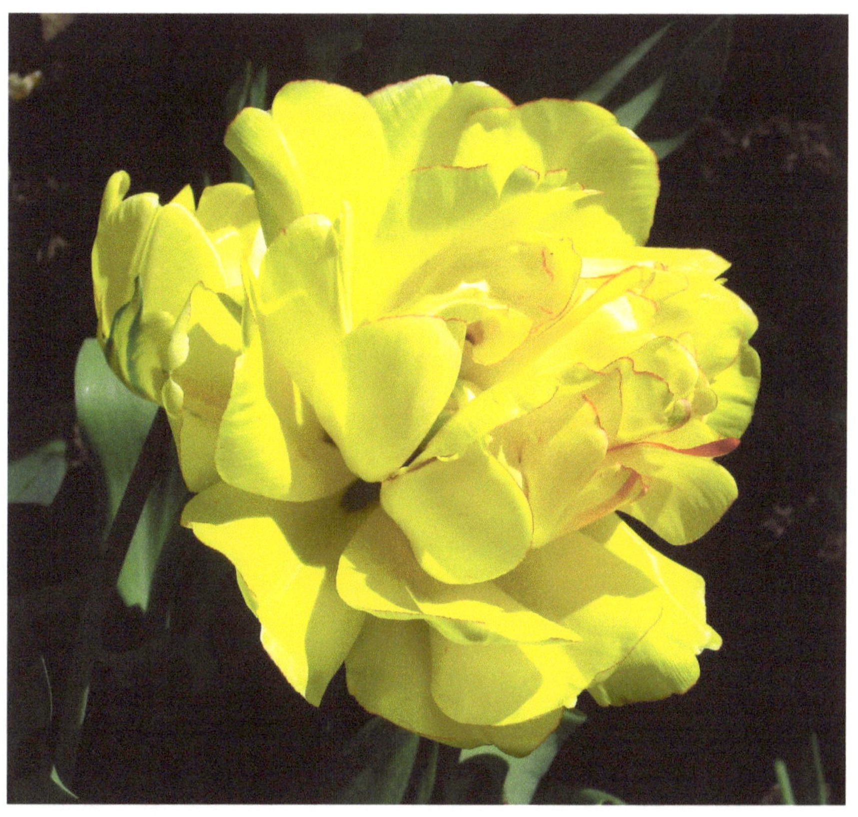